VOID

Library of
Davidson College

PUBLICATIONS
OF THE FACULTY OF ARTS
OF THE UNIVERSITY OF MANCHESTER
No. 23

THE VULGAR LATIN
of the letters
of Claudius Terentianus
(P. Mich. VIII, 467–72)

To my wife

THE VULGAR LATIN

❂

of the letters of Claudius Terentianus
(P. Mich. VIII, 467–72)

J. N. ADAMS

MANCHESTER
UNIVERSITY PRESS

© 1977 J. N. ADAMS

Published by
MANCHESTER UNIVERSITY PRESS
Oxford Road, Manchester M13 9PL

ISBN 0 7190 1289 9

BRITISH LIBRARY CATALOGUING IN PUBLICATION DATA

Adams, J N
  The vulgar Latin of the letters of Claudius
  Terentianus. – (University of Manchester.
  Faculty of Arts. Publications; no. 23).
  1. Terentianus, Claudius   2. Latin
  language, Vulgar – Usage
  I. Title   II. Terentianus, Claudius   III. Series
  477   PA2673

ISBN 0–7190–1289–9

Phototypeset by
Western Printing Services Ltd, Bristol
Printed in Great Britain by
The Pitman Press, Bath

CONTENTS

PREFACE *vii*

I INTRODUCTION *1*

II PHONOLOGY *7*

1 Vowels — *7*
2 Consonants — *22*

III MORPHOLOGY AND SYNTAX *36*

1 Case, prepositions and the nominal system — *36*
2 Pronouns — *44*
3 The verb — *48*
4 Conjunctions — *54*
5 Adjectives — *56*
6 Adverbs — *56*
7 Particles — *59*
8 Absolute constructions — *59*
9 Accusative and dative with the infinitive — *61*
10 Indirect questions — *64*
11 Negation — *65*

IV WORD ORDER *66*

1 Object position — *68*
2 The position of object pronouns — *69*
3 The genitive — *70*
4 Adjectives — *71*

5	The infinitive and embedded object sentences	71
6	Prepositional adjuncts	72
7	Relative clauses	72
8	Verb position	73
9	Subject, verb and object	74

V VOCABULARY 76

1	*aspros*	76
2	*byrrum*	77
3	*epistula*	77
4	*loncha*	77
5	*optio*	78
6	*paucum aes*	79
7	*fortis*	79
8	*iaceo*	79
9	*adiuto*	80
10	*uenio*	80
11	*palpo*	82
12	*pono*	82
13	*inuenio, reperio*	82
14	*praefuerunt*	82
15	*Puplicium*	83

VI CONCLUSION 84

APPENDIX: Changes in the vowel system 88

MODERN WORKS CITED 90

WORD INDEX 97

SUBJECT INDEX 99

PREFACE

The language of the Latin papyri has not attracted the attention it deserves. The status of Latin in Egypt was different from that in various other parts of the Empire, in that it was a minority language exposed to the influence of Greek. I have dealt elsewhere in more general terms (see the bibliography) with the Vulgar Latin of the early imperial papyri and with the question of bilingual interference in Egypt. Here I confine myself fairly strictly to the letters of Terentianus. The letters are both substantial in length and relatively early compared with most Vulgar Latin documents.

The manuscript was read by Professor H. D. Jocelyn and Professor V. Väänänen, to both of whom I am grateful for their care and for the suggestions that they made.

SYMBOLS

/ /	phoneme
[ ]	phonetic transcription
⟨ ⟩	grapheme

I INTRODUCTION

Evidence is notoriously short for the Vulgar Latin of the Republic and early Empire.[1] The satirists, comic poets and writers of mime undoubtedly used vulgarisms,[2] but all were men of learning who did not attempt a sustained imitation of the speech of the lower classes. Their work is as notable for parody of the higher literary forms and for comic neologisms as it is for Latin of colloquial flavour. Petronius set out to imitate vulgar speech in the *Cena Trimalchionis*,[3] but attempts by the educated to mimic social dialects which they themselves do not use are bound to contain a limited number of striking features to the exclusion of much else. There are many authentic syntactic and morphological vulgarisms in the *Cena*, but not much sign of the changes occurring in the sub-literate vowel system.

Inscriptions and graffiti (the most important of which are those found at Pompeii)[4] suffer from a different drawback. They may be written by the semi-literate, but inscriptions (notably those on tombs) are often formulaic, and graffiti are usually short. Neither type of document furnishes anything like an extensive corpus of one particular man's attempts at writing.

The letters of the soldier Claudius Terentianus (with which I include the one Latin letter of his father, Claudius Tiberianus)[5] are (along with the *Cena Trimalchionis* and the

[1] On the Republic, see now Campanile (1971), 1 ff.
[2] On the language of mime and Atellane farce, see Bonfante (1967).
[3] On the language of the *Cena*, see now Stefenelli (1962).
[4] On which see Väänänen (1966).
[5] The letters were first edited by Youtie and Winter (1951). They are reprinted in Cavenaile (1958), 250–55, and in Pighi (1964). Pighi has made

Pompeian material) the most important early example of
Vulgar Latin which has survived. Yet they have scarcely been
noticed by scholars. They were first discussed by Rita Calderini (1951) in a short article which is superficial and does no
justice to their importance. Pighi's commentary (1964) is
more reliable, but it too is brief, and it is also necessarily
unsystematic. Campanile refers often to the letters in his
recent discussion of the language of the Latin papyri (1971,
48 ff.), but he does little more than point out that some of the
phonological developments of Vulgar Latin are in evidence
there. As far as I know, the standard works on Vulgar Latin
and on Latin in general make no mention of the letters.[6]

The Latin of Egypt in general has been neglected, even
though the remains are substantial. Cavenaile's collection
(1958) of Latin papyri contains much (quite apart from the
letters of Terentianus) that should be of interest to students of
Vulgar Latin. Of particular note are the ostraca of Rustius
Barbarus found at Wâdi Fawâkhir (Nos. 303–9), which
belong to either the first or the second century. Two fourth
century bilingual glossaries throw light on both popular Latin
and Greek (277–8). Another military document remarkable
for its vulgarisms is 114 (A.D. 130). 40, a translation of parts of
the fables of Babrius, furnishes a glimpse of the Latin of a
Greek who had only a poor grasp of the language. In addition
to this material we have a letter from Oxyrhynchus recently
published by Virginia Brown (1970). And the Latin loan
words in Greek papyri also repay study, for they often reflect
a vulgar rather than an educated Latin base.[7] Although Egypt
does not have the same interest for linguists as the areas of the
Empire which were later to become Romance-speaking, the
speech community was unusual. Latin speakers learnt Greek,

a number of improvements to the text, which will be pointed out in due
course. An additional fragment has been published recently by Rodgers
(1970) (henceforth referred to as 5395).

[6] Hofmann and Szantyr (1965) and Väänänen (1967) do not appear to
exploit them.

[7] See the collections of loan words found in Meinersmann (1927),
Cavenaile (1951) and Daris (1960).

and Greeks undoubtedly learnt Latin (see below). In the speech of bilinguals each language must to some extent have interfered with the other.

It is clear from internal evidence that Terentianus was a soldier, and that as a veteran he later settled at Karanis.[8] The letters can be dated to the first quarter of the second century on the evidence of the handwriting, and there is also an allusion in one of them to events of A.D. 115.[9] They obviously cover a period of years. The hand varies because Terentianus made use of professional scribes,[10] but there is sufficient linguistic unity (see below, ch. VI) to show that the scribes did not make substantial changes in what was dictated to them.

Terentianus was a bilingual. He writes five times to his father in Latin and five times in Greek.[11] Taken together, the Greek and Latin letters provide a unique chance to compare Vulgar Latin and κοινή Greek. The features of both groups of letters are on the whole what might have been expected. But in Terentianus' Latin there are some signs of Greek interference, notably in word order (see below, ch. VI, for a summary of possible interference phenomena). Such interference is typical of the speech of bilinguals. Since we find no Latin interference in his Greek, it would seem that Greek was his usual language. But it would be misleading to imply that he was not completely fluent in Latin. His Latin contrasts sharply with that of the translation of Babrius mentioned above, in which Greek interference is apparent in almost every line.

It is curious that Terentianus writes to the same person, a member of his own family, in both Greek and Latin. Language switching within the family is typical of communities in which intermarriage commonly takes place between speakers of two different languages.[12] The offspring of such unions

[8] Youtie and Winter (1951), 17.
[9] Youtie and Winter (1951), 16; Pighi (1964), 4.
[10] Youtie and Winter (1951), *loc. cit.*
[11] See Youtie and Winter (1951), 476–80, for the Greek letters to Tiberianus. 481 (also in Greek) is to Tasoucharion.
[12] See Weinreich (1953), 84, for an example.

learn the two languages at the same time from their parents. The functions of the languages may come to overlap, though usually among bilinguals each language has a clearly delineated role. The Tiberianus archive seems to be the product of a special environment of this type. The Latin-speaking immigrants would not have been accompanied by many women. Intermarriage (or cohabitation) between Italians and local Greek women was inevitable, and from this bilingualism would have arisen. Since it is likely that many lower-class bilingual families were illiterate,[13] it is not surprising that written evidence of bilingualism is scarce. The letters, dictated as they were to scribes, form an isolated piece of evidence of extreme value.

Clearly it would be a mistake to argue from Greek ignorance of Latin literature (and the scarcity of Latin literary papyri before the fourth century seems to indicate that Latin literature was scarcely studied in Egypt in the early Empire)[14] that Greeks were also ignorant of the Latin language. A language exists mainly at the level of speech, even in a highly literate society. There must have been Greek-speakers in Egypt from the start of the Roman occupation who had a smattering of Vulgar Latin, if not a knowledge of Latin literature.[15]

The Latin letters are full of formulae which belonged not to the Latin but to the Greek epistolary style.[16] They clearly sprang from a society overwhelmingly Greek, in which some Greeks had become familiar with Latin. The Latin formula *si uales bene est, ego ualeo* described by Seneca as standard up to his day (*Epist.* 15.1) does not occur. Instead we find *ante omnia opto te bene [u]alere, que m[ihi ma]xime uota [su]nt* (468.3 f.), which corresponds to πρὸ μὲν πάντων εὔχομαί σε ὑγιαίνειν καὶ εὐτυχεῖν μοι, ὅ μοι εὐκταῖόν ἐστι (476.2; with the

---

[13] On illiteracy in Egypt, see, e.g., Youtie (1975).
[14] See Cameron (1970), 19 f.
[15] See Turner (1975) for some remarks on the interest among Greeks at Oxyrhynchus in things Roman.
[16] See Youtie and Winter (1951), 18. On Greek epistolary formulae in general in the papyri, see Exler (1923), Steen (1938).

dative *μοι* cf. *mihi* at 467.2 *an*[*te omn*]*ia op*[*to te*] *fortem et h*[*i*]*larem* [*e*]*t saluom mihi esse*). That the Latin expression was current in the epistolography of the area can be seen from the similar formula *opto deos ut bene ualeas que mea uota sunt* in a letter of Rustius Barbarus.[17] Other formulae are 468.46 *sal*[*u*]*tat te mater mea* (cf. 476.30 ἀσπάζεταί σε Ἐπιτυγχάνων), 468.61 *saluta omnes contubernales nostrous* (cf. 476.31 ἄσπασαι πάντες τοὺς φιλοῦντες [ἡμᾶς]), 468.64 *bene ualere te opto multis annis* (cf. 477.44 f. ἐρρῶσ]θ[αί σε] εὔχομαι πολ[λοῖς χ]ρό[νοις]),[18] and 467.4 *scias . . . pater* (cf. 466.5 γεινώσκειν σε θέλω, πατήρ).

It may well be that early imperial Latin papyri, including our letters, will cause a revision of views about classical orthography. Even vulgar documents are remarkable for conservatism of spelling. The Augustan letter published by Brown (1970), for instance, shows the original diphthongal spelling *tibei*,[19] *deuom* = *diuorum* (where ⟨e⟩ represents the old Latin phoneme /ẹ̄/),[20] *uolt* = *uult* (see below, II.1.i), and the school spelling *qum* (see below, II.2.vi.). In a second or third century declamatory exercise (Cavenaile (1958), 65) long vowels are marked by an *apex* and /ī/ is rendered by ⟨ei⟩ (for which spelling see below, II.1.ii). Similar conservatism in Terentianus will be pointed out in the course of this work (for a summary of the evidence, see ch. VI).

There can scarcely be a vulgar text extant which is free of hyperurbanisms and attempts at formality. No one writes as he speaks. A poorly educated writer will employ a mixture of current vulgarisms and learned usages (often misunderstood) which he has picked up. The letters of Terentianus, however, are relatively free of hyperurbanisms. Perhaps because he was dictating rather than composing with a pen in his hand, Terentianus made no attempt to impart a stylistic formality.

---

[17] See Cavenaile (1958), 304.2.
[18] Notice that in both Latin and Greek the governing verb follows the acc. + infin. This position is abnormal in the Latin letters (see below, IV.5), and must therefore have been determined by the formulaic order.
[19] For which see Ernout (1953), 147.
[20] For which see Sturtevant (1940), 114 f.

Letter 471 is especially noteworthy. It contains a heated account of a quarrel described with a liberal use of direct speech. There is no sign at all of stylistic elaboration.

The Latin letters not only provide abundant confirmation of many of the trends of Vulgar Latin. On certain points they cause us either to modify the traditional chronology (based often on much later evidence) or to reject the traditional explanation of a phenomenon. The most important evidence which they furnish will be summarised at the end (ch. vi).

II PHONOLOGY

1 VOWELS

i Restructuring of the vowel system

The Latin letters show clear signs of the vowel changes which accompanied the loss of phonemic quantitative distinctions in Vulgar Latin,[1] just as the Greek letters have non-classical spellings which reflect the vowel system of κοινή Greek.[2] It is the falling together of /ē/ and /i/ which is most apparent.[3] In most vulgar texts, alongside the representation of classical /i/ by means of ⟨e⟩, there are usually inverse examples of ⟨i⟩ for /ē/ which are often difficult to interpret.[4] But the letters are remarkable in that there are no aberrational spellings of this type.[5]

[1] Cf. Calderini (1951), 252.
[2] For the confusion of ⟨o⟩ and ⟨ω⟩ caused by the loss of quantitative distinctions, see 476.18 ζοῆς = ζωῆς. On this confusion see Meillet (1965), 283 f.; Mayser (1906–34), I, 98 f. Note especially the orthographic alternation of ⟨ει⟩ and ⟨ι⟩: e.g. 476.18 ἀκείνητος = ἀκίνητος, 477.18 f. γράφις = γράφεις, 479.10 ἀναδώσις = ἀναδώσεις, 481.8 ἀντιγράψις = ἀντιγράψεις. Spellings of this type are common from the second century B.C. onwards (Meillet (1965), 259; Mayser (1906–34), I, 87 ff.).
[3] On which see, e.g., Bourciez (1946), 42 f.; B. Löfstedt (1961), 21. See also below, Appendix (88 f.).
[4] B. Löfstedt (1961), 21 ff.
[5] It is conceivable that at 470.24 in an obscure context there is an anomalous example of ⟨i⟩ for /e/ (beni = bene?), but it is more likely that beni is either an imperative (cf. 471.33 ueni, dicet, where the phraseology seems to be the same as at 470.24) or a perfect (cf. 471.17). There is possibly one other aberrational spelling involving the grapheme ⟨e⟩. At 471.12 the editors read ⟨h⟩inc ebinde, taking ebinde as equivalent to abinde. There is no satisfactory linguistic explanation for this form. Pighi's comment 'La grafia inc ebinde è fonetica' (1964, 68) is obscure. It seems

The examples of ⟨e⟩ for /i/ are as follows:

468.35 nese = nisi
468.38 sene = sine (cf. OSp. *sene*, OLog. *sene*)[6]
468.38 uolueret = uoluerit
468.40 nesi = nisi
468.41 aiutaueret = aiutauerit
471.11 lentiamina = linteamina[7]
471.33 dicet = dicit
471.34 lentiamina
5395.10 nese

At 469.18 *illec* probably stands for *illaec* (see III.2.i), but the passage is so fragmentary that it could represent *illic*. If so the vowel change would be the same as those above.

At 471.29 *xylesphongium* for the usual Greek ξυλοσφόγγιον may be explained as a rendition of a Greek by-form ξυλεσφόγγιον (so Youtie and Winter (1951), 39). Alternatively it is possible that the standard linking morph -*i*- of Latin compounds, represented as ⟨e⟩ (= /ẹ/) has replaced the Greek ⟨o⟩. For similar replacement, cf. *Appendix Probi* 22 *aquae ductus non aquiductus*; 159 *terrae motus non terrimotium*; *SHA, Firm.* 8.6 *linifio* = λινόυφος.

The spellings *uendedi*⟨t⟩ (471.34) and *uendedi* (472.8) are not phonetically determined but due to recomposition.[8] Cf. 468.39 f. *commandaticiae*, with which compare *CIL* VI.10464 *commando* (cf. It. *comando*).[9]

About a third of the examples listed above are verb forms

---

highly likely that Terentianus intended *hinc ed inde*, an expression which would give perfect sense: *hinc ed inde collexi paucum aes* = 'I collected a little money from here and there' (for *hinc et inde*, see *TLL* VI.3.2805.44 ff.; it occurs at *Per. Aeth.* 45.2, *Vit. Patr.* 5.15.46 and often in Latin of all types). The letters often have *ed* for *et*. Either the editors misread *b* for *d*, or the scribe made a slip.

[6] See Meyer-Lübke (1935), 7936.

[7] Cf. *Vita Seruatii* 1.3; Schuchardt (1866–68), I, 438, II, 56. Cf. *linteum* > Cat. *llens* (Meyer-Lübke (1935), 5072).

[8] For recomposed perfects in -*dedi*, see Carlton (1973), 45; Vielliard (1927), 168 f. On recomposition in general, see B. Löfstedt (1961), 182 ff.

[9] Cf. Calderini (1951), 252. Pighi (1964), 54 f., oddly denies that *commandaticiae* is due to recomposition. He has nothing to say on *uendedi*.

exhibiting the merger of /ē/ and /i/ in final syllable. Such forms are also common at Pompeii: e.g. *CIL* IV.6825 *bibet*, 9167 *colet*, 5370 *contemnet*.[10] Väänänen (1966, 22; cf. 130) is inclined to interpret them as due to substrate influence (that of Oscan). He warns against putting spellings such as *dicet* at Pompeii on the same footing as identical spellings found in late Latin. But the presence of forms of the same type in the letters as early as the start of the second century suggests that they could have been due even at Pompeii to a genuine Latin readjustment in the vowel system. So in the ostraca of Rustius Barbarus *scribes* and *mittes* are written for *scribis* and *mittis*.[11] The profusion of forms with *-et* for *-it* at Pompeii and elsewhere is no doubt due partly to the fact that in final syllables distinctions of quantity were more easily obscured than elsewhere in the word, and partly to the analogical influence of the large number of verbs (of the second declension) which regularly had the grapheme ⟨e⟩ in their final syllable in the present indicative.

There are thus between nine and eleven spellings reflecting the change /i/ > /ę/, most of which are in unstressed syllables. It is likely that the blurring of quantitative distinctions and the consequent vowel mergers first took place in unstressed syllables.[12]

The use of the grapheme ⟨o⟩ for /u/ is superficially more common than the use of ⟨e⟩ for /i/, but almost every example is a special case. Usually spellings with ⟨o⟩ for /u/ are found in words in which /o/ had been original before the change of /o/ > /u/ in certain environments.[13] In such circumstances it is possible either that the spelling is deliberately archaising and has no phonetic basis, or that the change /o/ > /u/ had not fully taken place. It is difficult to determine whether we are faced by a recently emerged vulgarism or an archaising tendency. In the absence of unambiguous examples which could

---

[10] Väänänen (1966), 22.   [11] See Cavenaile (1958), 304.3, 4.
[12] The majority of the examples of ⟨e⟩ for /i/ noted by Väänänen (1966), 21 f., are in unstressed, and particularly final, syllables.
[13] This is also the case at Pompeii: Väänänen (1966), 27.

not be interpreted as displaying an archaising spelling, we should not be justified in treating non-classical forms as evidence for the vulgar merger of /ō/ and /u/.[14]

After both /u/ and /w/ the change /o/ > /u/ took place later than elsewhere.[15] In four places it is in just this environment that ⟨o⟩ for /u/ occurs: 467.2 *saluom*, 467.4 *nouom*, 467.17 *fugitiuom*, 469.8 *bolt* = *uolt*.[16] Even if /o/ had closed in this position by this time, spelling is slow to be affected by changes in pronunciation. We certainly could not argue that these forms reflect the falling together of /ō/ and /u/.

Many of the examples of ⟨o⟩ for /u/ are accounted for by the form *con* = *cum* (468.12, 50, 51, 52, 53, 54, 55, 57, 61, 471.23, 32). The vowel appears to be that of Romance reflexes such as It., Sp. *con*,[17] but it could also be that of old Latin forms of the word (see Prisc. *GL* III.39.16 *antiqui . . . pro cum com scribebant*). So at Pompeii *com* (*CIL* IV.3935) and *quom* (conjunction: 1654, 1846, 5269; this form is definitely archaising) occur.[18] It is safest to assume that the spelling with ⟨o⟩ is archaising, though it is impossible to be sure. In later Latin, when /ō/ and /u/ had definitely merged, the form *con* is very common in inscriptions.[19] For another archaising spelling (differing in type) of this preposition, see 469.6 *qumqupibit* (on which see II.2.vi).

According to the editors, *sopera* (471.21) is an old form. It is true that *supra* is an original feminine ablative of *superus* and that the form *supera* without syncope is attested (e.g. Liv. Andr. 3 *mea puera quid uerbi ex tuo ore supera fugit?*). But /o/ is not the original vowel of the word. In this case there are stronger grounds for believing that the spelling is due to the

---

[14] On this merger, see, e.g., Bourciez (1946), 42 f.; B. Löfstedt (1961), 21.

[15] See Buck (1933), 83. Buck states that 'the earliest example of *u* in such cases is *suum* beside *suom* in an inscription of 45 B.C., and the spelling *o* is often found much later, especially in *volt*, *volnus*'.

[16] Cf. Väänänen (1966), 28 (for examples of *uolt*).

[17] On the retention of a final nasal in monosyllables, see Bourciez (1946), 48; Väänänen (1967), 69 f.

[18] Väänänen (1966), 28.   [19] Väänänen (1966), *loc. cit.*

falling together of /ō/ and /u/ as /ǫ/ (cf. It. *sopra*).[20] But the absence of syncope scarcely reflects the popular language. Terentianus may have contaminated *supra* with *super*.[21]

Finally, *quominos* at 470.26 again seems to have an archaising spelling.[22]

On *pulbin[o]* (468.12), see below, III.1.i, and so on *posso* (469.15), see III.3.iv.

In vulgar texts from most areas ⟨e⟩ is written for /i/ considerably more often than ⟨o⟩ for /u/,[23] and it is likely that the merger of /ō/ and /u/ was later than that of /ē/ and /i/.[24] In the Romania the convergence of /ō/ and /u/ is not as complete as that of /ē/ and /i/.[25] In our letters ⟨e⟩ for /i/ is more securely attested than ⟨o⟩ for /u/. Moreover a further argument will be given below suggesting that the merger of /ō/ and /u/ had scarcely begun (II.2.i).

The importance of the letters is that they make it certain that the falling together of /ē/ and /i/ had begun by the first century. Previously the Pompeian evidence was suspect because of the possibility of substrate influence.

There is no sign of hypercorrect inverse spellings, but the scribes show a marked tendency to write ⟨o⟩ for /u/ in environments in which /o/ had been original. Since comparable spellings abound at Pompeii, it seems likely that the old orthography was widely taught in the schools.

ii Diphthongs

The diphthong /au/, which still survives today in part of the Romania,[26] occurs twenty-six times in the letters. It is never monophthongised.

On the other hand there is plentiful evidence of the monophthongisation of /ae/.[27] Though spellings with the

---

[20] For other examples with the vowel ⟨o⟩, see Schuchardt (1866–68), II, 158.   [21] Cf. Pighi (1964), 70.   [22] Cf. Calderini (1951), 253.
[23] B. Löfstedt (1961), 90.   [24] Väänänen (1966), 27.
[25] Bourciez (1946), 43. See, however, Gaeng (1968), 83 f., 97 ff., on the special frequency of ⟨o⟩ for /u/ in Christian inscriptions from central Italy.
[26] See, e.g., Väänänen (1966), 30.
[27] On which see B. Löfstedt (1961), 102; Coleman (1971).

diphthong are slightly more numerous than those with ⟨e⟩ (21:18; in the great majority of vulgar texts the conservatism of writing ensures that the diphthong is far more predominant than this), the incidence of ⟨e⟩ is enough to suggest that in the spoken registers /ae/ had been monophthongised completely.

Once /ae/ had been monophthongised, we should expect the use of the grapheme ⟨ae⟩ to be determined by the orthographic rules operating on the writer. In late Italian texts ⟨ae⟩ is more often written in the prefix *prae-* and in the case inflections than in initial and medial positions of the word.[28] This is because it could readily be learnt that ⟨ae⟩ had a place in certain defunct case endings and after *pr-*, whereas no single rule could instruct the writer when the diphthong should be employed in other parts of the word: hence phonetic spellings predominate there. In the letters ⟨ae⟩ is never reduced in the prefix (468.30 *praestat*, *praeterea*, 471.19 *praegnatam*), but ⟨e⟩ does occur in case inflections. But seven of the nine examples are in the word *Alexandrie* (470.19, 471.15, 22, 25, 32, 33, 35; cf. *magne* 469.9, *mee* 471.16), which to judge by its use had been fossilised in this area as a locative-directional (see III.1.ii). It must have been in constant use, and hence it was written with a phonetic spelling. But in words less regularly used with genitive, dative or locative inflections the scribes remembered to employ the learned grapheme ⟨ae⟩.[29]

There is one example of *Alexandriae*, but that is in the letter of Tiberianus (472.9). Tiberianus seems to have had greater stylistic pretensions than Terentianus. He alone employs the ablative absolute (9 f. *occasione inuenta*), and he also uses *reperio* (19 f.), whereas Terentianus always has the everyday *inuenio*. Note too the archaic form *abs* (3).

The letters provide no evidence for the form which the monophthongisation took.[30] The only inverse spelling which they contain is ⟨ae⟩ for /e/ at 469.11 (*resc̣reibae*).

---

[28] See Adams (1976), 43 ff.
[29] For the other examples of ⟨e⟩, see 468.3, 471.14 *que*, 471.17 *Ptolemes*, 469.18 *illec*, 469.4, 8, 13, 14, 18 *illei* = *illaei* (on which see below, III.2.i).
[30] On this question see Coleman (1971).

At 468.62 *nostrous* (= *nostros*) is obviously a Grecism (see the editors *ad loc*.).

The use of ⟨ei⟩ for /ī/ seen in *rescreibae* (469.11) is common in inscriptions.[31]

iii Opening caused by /r/

From the earliest period in Latin /r/ showed a tendency either to open the preceding vowel or to prevent its closing.[32] In the prehistoric period in unstressed open syllables /a/ usually proceeded to /i/ (e.g. in *conficio* alongside *facio*), but if it was followed by /r/ the closing stopped half way at /e/. Hence the perfect of *pario* is *peperi* rather than *pepiri (cf. *reddere* alongside *dare*). So the name *Numasius*, which occurs on the Praenestine fibula (*CIL* I².3), became *Numerius* after rhotacism rather than *Numirius*.

The editors have no explanation of *itarum* = *iterum* (468.23), and Calderini (1951, 252) merely asserts that in an unstressed syllable the vowel has become uncertain. Pighi (1964, 51) says that *itarum* is a 'grafia fonetica', but does not explain.

Itarum presents a clear case of opening before /r/.[33] There is abundant evidence that the tendency persisted in Vulgar Latin, though often a form of this type is susceptible of another explanation. Thus *marcator*, *marcatus*, *lauaratum*, *martarium* and *camara*, which will be dealt with below (II.1.iv), are perhaps due to vocalic assimilation.

In the *Appendix Probi* a number of words are censured which contain -*ar* rather than -*er* in the termination: 43 *carcer non carcar*, 163 *passer non passar*, 164 *anser non ansar*.[34] Väänänen (1967, 36) regards the opening as caused by /ɪ/,

---

[31] Väänänen (1966), 22. It was an orthographic attempt to render the long vowel made possible by the falling together of /ei/ and /ī/. Cf. Coleman (1963), 3.   [32] Palmer (1954), 219.

[33] Cf. Campanile (1971), 55. So too at 468.12 the scribe first wrote *emaram* before correcting to *emeram* (Pighi (1964), 47).

[34] To these could be added *lasar* (see Schuchardt (1866–68), I, 208; Baehrens (1922), 29) and *assar* (Schuchardt (1866–68), I, 206; Baehrens (1922), *loc. cit.*; cf. Sen. *assaro*: Meyer-Lübke (1935), 725).

and he may be partially right. But in each case the stressed vowel is /a/, and hence here too there may have been assimilation.

Another determinant is also possible in the case of *nouarca* = *nouerca* (*App. Prob.* 168). Baehrens (1922, 30) argues that a popular etymology caused the change: see Festus 181.3 L *nouerca dicitur, quam quis liberis sublatis nouam uxorem ducit arcendae familiae gratia*.

But no other determinant could have produced *libartis* (*CIL* VI.10104b).[35] So *ualeriana* (a type of fig) survived as Abbruz. *vaiarane*,[36] *lacertus* ('upper arm') as Sp. and Pg. *lagarto*,[37] *pergaminum* ('parchment') as Log. *bargaminu* and Prov. *pargamí*,[38] *seruiens* as Sp. *sargento* and Pg. *sargente*,[39] and *eruilia* as Emil. *arviya* and Sp. *arveja*.[40] A number of Latin loan words in Welsh derive from forms in which opening of /e/ to /a/ before /r/ had taken place: *tafarn* < *tabarna, *sarff* < *sarpens.[41] Finally, Schuchardt (1886–68) quotes examples of *sarra* = *sera* (I, 210), *oparue* = *operae* (I, 206), *pareat* = *pereat* (*loc. cit.*) and *Tarentinus* = *Terentinus* (I, 207).

iv Assimilation of vowels

According to the editors[42] *dalabra* = *dolabra* (468.27) is exceptional, for elsewhere the word exhibits only progressive assimilation.[43] But in reality the form is due to what was probably the most common type of vocalic assimilation in Vulgar Latin. It frequently happens that a pre-tonic vowel is assimilated to the following accented vowel (regressive), or alternatively a post-tonic vowel is occasionally assimilated to the preceding accented vowel (progressive).[44] Vocalic assimi-

---

[35] Quoted by Väänänen (1967), 36.   [36] Meyer-Lübke (1935), 9130 *a*.
[37] Meyer-Lübke (1935), 4822.   [38] Meyer-Lübke (1935), 6411.
[39] Meyer-Lübke (1935), 7873.   [40] Meyer-Lübke (1935), 2909.
[41] Campanile (1969), 103. Jackson's suggestion (1953, 83) that 'it may be that *er* > *ar* was more characteristic of the Latin of Britain than of the Continent' can be rejected.
[42] Cf. Pighi (1964), 52.   [43] For *dolobra*, see Baehrens (1922), 26.
[44] A few examples are given by Rohlfs (1949–53), I, 527 f.; Meyer-Lübke (1890–1906), I, §359; Bourciez (1946), 158; Carlton (1973), 198.

lation in Latin is nowhere treated other than cursorily, nor is it usual for any one type to be distinguished from another. It is therefore worthwhile to establish the importance of the type exemplified by *dalabra*. I have collected numerous examples, most of which are regressive:

danarius = *denarius*: > OIt. *danaio*.[45]
saluaticus = *siluaticus*: used by Anthimus (86), and also attested in the Reichenau Glosses. It survives in Prov. *salvatge*, Fr. *sauvage*, Rum. *salbatic*, etc.[46]
tanaculum = *tenaculum*: > It. *tanaglia*, etc. (but Fr. *tenailles*).[47]
balancia = *bilancia*: this word replaced *libra*. It is reflected in Fr. as *balance* and in Prov. and Cat. as *balansa* (but cf. It. *bilancia*).[48]
monistirium = *monasterium*: the ⟨i⟩ of the antepenult represents the pronunciation in late Greek of η. To this the preceding unstressed vowel was sometimes assimilated (*TLL* VIII.1402.65 f.).
ergesterium = *ergasterium*: found at Diom. *GL* 1.492.6 (*B*).
tolonium = *telonium* (τελώνιον): the learned form *telonium* is used by Tertullian and in the Vulgate. The assimilated form is censured at *App. Prob.* 2. Only the latter survives in Romance (OFr. *tonlieu*).[49]
imbilicus = *umbilicus*: so *App. Prob.* 58. Cf. Log. *imbíligu*.[50] But here it is impossible to decide between two determinants. The first syllable may have been interpreted as the prefix *in-* (with assimilation to the following labial).
mataxa = *metaxa* (μέταξα): *mataxa* is found as early as Lucilius (1192), and it is reflected in Romance (It. *matassa*).[51] But the base form is uncertain, for μάταξα is also attested in Greek.

[45] Meyer-Lübke (1935), 2553. Cf. Grandgent (1927), 43, on Tuscan dialects.
[46] Meyer-Lübke (1935), 7922. Cf. Rohlfs (1949–53), I, 527; Meyer-Lübke (1890–1906), I, §359; Bourciez (1946), 158.
[47] Meyer-Lübke (1935), 8637.
[48] Meyer-Lübke (1935), 1103. Cf. Bourciez (1946), 158.
[49] Meyer-Lübke (1935), 8622. Cf. Baehrens (1922), 27.
[50] Meyer-Lübke (1935), 9045.   [51] Meyer-Lübke (1935), 5403.

referandarius = *referendarius*: an example of the former is given by Vielliard (1927, 22), who, however, describes it as 'une erreur accidentelle due à la pronunciation voisine de *e* et *a* non accentués devant nasale'. There is no need to invoke the influence of the nasal. It is the following vowel that has caused the spelling.

tramaculum = *tremaculum*: the form with assimilation lies behind Ven. *tramaǧo*, Tarent. *tramaggya*, Pg. *tramalho*.[52]

piatatem = *pietatem*: this form is demanded by Prov. *piatat*, Sic. *piatá*.[53] With this should be compared an example of *ueratatis* = *ueritatis* quoted by Schuchardt (1866–68, I, 219).

cucuta = *cicuta*: > Rum. *cucută*. Found at Pompeii (*CIL* IV.8065, 8066).[54]

parantalia = *parentalia*: censured at *App. Prob.* 183.

aramen = *aeramen*: > Rum. *aramă*, Sp. *alambre*, Prov. *aram*.[55]

tugurium: treated by Baehrens (1922, 33) as an example of assimilation (<*tegurium*), but the attachment of the word to *tego* may be a popular etymology.[56]

lucusta = *locusta*: see *CGL* III.44.15.[57]

butumen = *bitumen*: censured at *App. Prob.* 193.

*gagantem = *gigantem*: > OFr. *jaint*, Prov. *jaian*.[58]

There are also various forms containing ⟨a⟩ before /r/ which could have been produced by assimilation, or perhaps the /r/ opened the vowel (the two factors are not mutually exclusive). *Veruactum* is reflected as Log. *barvattu*,[59] and both *marcator* = *mercator*[60] and *marcatus* = *mercatus*[61] survive (e.g. OFr. *marcheour*, Fr. *marché*).

To these examples could be added many comparable forms which are scattered throughout Schuchardt. Some may contain haphazard scribal errors, but in other cases an aberra-

---

[52] Meyer-Lübke (1935), 8875.   [53] Meyer-Lübke (1935), 6485.
[54] See Baehrens (1922), 32; Battisti (1949), 114; Väänänen (1966), 26.
[55] Meyer-Lübke (1935), 242. Cf. Bourciez (1946), 158.
[56] Ernout and Meillet (1959), *s.v.*
[57] See Schuchardt (1866–68), II, 109.
[58] Meyer-Lübke (1935), 3758. Cf. Meyer-Lübke (1890–1906), I, §359.
[59] Meyer-Lübke (1935), 9264.   [60] Meyer-Lübke (1935), 5515 *b*.
[61] Meyer-Lübke (1935), 5516.

tional spelling may be due to the isolated working of assimilation. I record the following examples without comment: *lauaratum* = *laboratum* (Schuchardt (1866–68) I, 172), *onnorum* = *annorum* (I, 173), *lucuna* = *lacuna*, *lucunar* = *lacunar* (I, 174), *martarium* = *mortarium* (I, 184), *congragati* = *congregati* (I, 213), *existamauerit* = *existimauerit* (I, 217), *siruitium* = *seruitium* (I, 358), *perigrina* = *peregrina* (I, 387), *rutundus* = *rotundus* (II, 141), *suggultium* = *singultus* (II, 234).

I conclude with a few examples of the rarer phenomenon of progressive assimilation to the stressed vowel:

colober, colobra = *coluber, colubra*: see *App. Prob.* 177 *coluber non colober*; cf. *CGL* IV.500.26 *colober ab eo est dictus quod colit umbras*.[62]

colop(h)us = *colaphus* (κόλαφος): for the form with assimilation, see *CGL* III.351.23, IV.181.15. Petronius has a denominative based on it (44.5 *percolopare*, in a speech by a freedman).[63]

aradam = *aridam*: an example is given by Schuchardt (1866–68, I, 217).

tonotrus = *tonitrus*: found at *App. Prob.* 162. According to Baehrens (1922, 35) this form is not due to assimilation but is onomatopoeic ('das doppelte *o* das dunkle Rollen des Donners wiedergeben soll'). But it is unjustified to rule out either of the possible determinants.

oppodum = *oppidum*: found in an early inscription (*CIL* I².585.81).[64]

solodus = *solidus*: an example is given by Schuchardt (1866–68, II, 251).

camara = *camera*: the latter was preferred in educated Latin, but *camara* is nevertheless common.[65] Both are reflected in Romance (It. *camera*, Sp., Pg. *camara*). But again it is possible that the second vowel was opened by the /r/.

---

[62] For the Romance reflexes of the assimilated form, see Gröber (1884), 550.
[63] Stefenelli (1962), 45 f. Cf. Baehrens (1922), 26.
[64] See Schuchardt (1866–68), II, 251; Baehrens (1922), 35.
[65] See, e.g., Baehrens (1922), 37.

v Hiatus and contraction

Both /e/ and /i/ in hiatus before a more open vowel developed into /j/: cf. It. *figlia* < *filia* alongside *paglia* < *palea*.[66] At Pompeii and elsewhere there are numerous examples of ⟨i⟩ for classical /e/ in hiatus[67] which are difficult to interpret. Except at Pompeii the misspelling is rare until late Latin.[68] But at Pompeii the possibility of Oscan influence must be considered.[69] Moreover many examples could be interpreted as due to a change of suffix (e.g. *-ia* for *-ea*, *-iolus* for *-eolus*). One might be tempted to believe that the genuine phonetic change took place much later.

However, it is not possible to draw a distinction between the nature of the early and of the later evidence. Though many cases of ⟨i⟩ for /e/ at Pompeii could be due to a change of suffix, the same is true of most examples from later Latin.[70] Moreover it is a remarkable fact that while ⟨i⟩ is written for /e/ very often at Pompeii and elsewhere, ⟨e⟩ is rarely written for /i/.[71] If we had to do merely with haphazard changes of suffix, we should expect ⟨e⟩ for /i/ to be more common.

In the letters of Terentianus ⟨i⟩ for /e/ occurs five times.[72]

---

[66] Väänänen (1966), 34, (1967), 46.

[67] For the many examples of this type in the *Appendix Probi*, see Baehrens (1922), 38.

[68] Väänänen (1966), 36. But against this view, see Campanile (1971), 28 ff.

[69] Väänänen (1966), *loc. cit.*

[70] See the examples given by Schuchardt (1866–68), I, 424 ff., and Vielliard (1927), 21.

[71] In the *Appendix Probi* ⟨i⟩ for /e/ is censured fourteen times, but ⟨e⟩ for /i/ only four times (Baehrens (1922), 38). Väänänen (1966, 36 f.) quotes some eighty examples of ⟨i⟩ for /e/ at Pompeii, compared with only about eleven of ⟨e⟩ for /i/. Vielliard (1927, 21) gives forty-four examples of ⟨i⟩ for /e/ (only a selection of instances), against nine of ⟨e⟩ for /i/. In the Spanish inscriptions ⟨e⟩ for /i/ appears to predominate, but the great majority of examples are in barbarous proper names, the base forms of which are of course uncertain (Carnoy (1906), 42). In the Ravenna Papyri change in hiatus is rarely attested (Carlton (1973), 105). The examples given from Gregory of Tours by Bonnet (1890), 114, 118 are selective.

[72] Though numerically not impressive, these examples could not all be due to scribal slips.

Here obviously we do not have to reckon with the possibility of Oscan influence. The presence of the phenomenon in the letters lends support to the view that Oscan influence need not be invoked to account for the Pompeian examples. Moreover since ⟨e⟩ for /i/ does not occur, it is preferable to explain the spellings phonologically rather than morphologically.

It is impossible to tell whether ⟨i⟩ represents /j/ or a closer articulation of the vowel. But it does seem likely that closing was an intermediate stage in the consonification of /e/ in hiatus.[73]

The ⟨i⟩ of *uitriae* = *uitreae* (468.17) could only represent a close vowel, for the preceding consonant would have prevented yodisation. Cf. *creare* > It. *criare*, Sp. *criar*.[74] With *calcio* = *calceo* (468.26) compare *App. Prob.* 81 *calceus non calcius*, and with *lentiamina* = *linteamina* (471.11, 34) cf. *App. Prob.* 157 *linteum non lintium*,[75] *P. Oxy.* 929 λέντιον = *linteum*. The other example is *linium* = *lineum* (5395.3).

The treatment of /i/ in hiatus in the letters is peculiar. In the case of *anaboladum* = *anaboladium* (467.5) we should have expected an additional grapheme after ⟨d⟩. If this example stood alone, it could be regarded as a scribal error (as indeed it is regarded by the editors). But there is a parallel at 470.11 (*aduuabat* = *adiuuabat*), though of course the ⟨i⟩ had always represented [j]. The two examples of *aiuto* = *adiuto* (468.41, 471.28; cf. It. *aiutare*) are also relevant.

When /i/ in hiatus developed to /j/ the original stop was palatalised, though the exact nature of the palatalisation is unclear. There were probably variations according to social class, period and area. Then the palatalised consonant in some areas opened to /j/.[76] The intermediate stage, whatever its nature, defied precise orthographic representation, and it is this which caused variations of spelling. Väänänen (1966,

---

[73] See Väänänen (1966), 34.   [74] Väänänen (1966), *loc. cit.*
[75] For an example of *lentiamina*, see Bonnet (1890), 114.
[76] See Väänänen (1967), 55; Grandgent (1927), 68 f., 92 f., 101 f.; Pope (1934), 129, 131.

35 f.) deals with two variant spellings at Pompeii which reflect the difficulty (the use of *I longa*, and gemination of the consonant in an attempt to render the palatalisation), and a third might also be stressed. Sometimes at Pompeii and elsewhere ⟨i⟩ is omitted in hiatus after stops in the same way as in the letters (e.g. the Pompeian *auctone* and *sexages*;[77] cf. Diehl (1910) 196 *des* = *dies*, *CIL* VI.10238 *custoda*, 10329 *sortitone*, *P. Ryl.* 225 πάκτωνος = *pactionis*?), and no doubt for the same reason: though the palatalisation could not be accurately rendered, the syllabic reduction caused by the consonification of /i/ would at least receive recognition if ⟨i⟩ were deleted. Compare the frequent omission of ⟨i⟩ in *filius*, *-a* (Diehl (1910) 29, 75, 337, 1439; cf. 188 *aleno* = *alieno*, 1362 *abalenare*, *CIL* XIII.2189 *laesone* = *laesione*).

The form *aiuto* (contrasting with *aduuabat*) indicates that usage was in state of flux or indeterminacy between the second and third stages.

When two juxtaposed vowels are of the same or similar quality, contraction is the rule.[78] *Dende* (= *deinde*) at 471.19, a form widely reflected in Romance (e.g. Sp., OPg. *dende*),[79] should certainly be retained, though the editors regularise.[80] The original /i/ of the second syllable would have developed regularly to /ẹ/ (cf. *inde* > OSp., OPg. *ende*).[81] *Deinde* is attested with /ē/ in the first syllable, the reflex of which would also have been /ẹ/. Alternatively, if *dēinde* does not lie behind the contracted form, short /e/ (VL /ę/) might have contracted, with the outcome of classical /i/ (VL /ẹ/).

Mihi is contracted to *mi* eleven times. The full form is found nineteen times. There are variations of practice from letter to letter. In 467 *mihi* occurs ten times, *mi* never, whereas in 471 *mi* is preferred by 6:1. It has already been mentioned that 471 is notable for its quotations of direct speech and its heated

---

[77] Väänänen (1966), 40.
[78] See, e.g., Väänänen (1967), 45.
[79] Meyer-Lübke (1935), 2525.
[80] But Pighi (1964), 70, favours its retention.
[81] Meyer-Lübke (1935), 4368.

tone. It is likely that it gives us a closer glimpse of the spoken language than any of the other letters. Terentianus perhaps took care to dictate the learned form in 467, but in 471 dropped the attempt (for an alternative explanation see below, ch. vi). In the letter of Tiberianus (whose stylistic aspirations we have referred to) *mihi* only is used (472.12, 17).

With *mi* we might compare *nil* = *nihil* at 471.19. At 470.23 *denaris* = *denariis* would be comparable with Pompeian examples such as *Fabis* = *Fabiis* (*CIL* iv.1087, 1095, etc.) and *iudicis* = *iudiciis* (528),[82] but the editors find space for a missing letter.

Of particular note are the spellings *ma* (471.34), *tus* (471.17) and *sum* (471.30) for *mea*, *tuus* and *suum*, all of which are regularised by the editors. The contracted forms *sus*, *tus* and *mus* are all attested and reflected in Romance.[83] Note that all three vulgarisms are in 471.

On *Ptolemes* (a Grecising spelling) at 471.21, see the editors *ad loc.*

vi Syncope

Syncope is common in the letters.[84] I list the relevant examples without comment: 467.6, 9 *aspros* (on which see below, v.1), 467.23 *postae*,[85] 467.20 *coplam*, 468.10 *amicla*, 468.14 f. *singlare*, 469.2 *sitlas*, 468.6 *uetranum*.

vii Aphaeresis

According to Calderini (1951, 259) *spectemus* = *exspectemus* at 471.24 is a simplex used instead of the compound. But in fact it is an early example of aphaeresis.[86] *Specto* in this sense

---

[82] Väänänen (1966), 39.
[83] Meyer-Lübke (1935), 5556, 8493 a, 9020; Carnoy (1906), 113; Grandgent (1907), 95; Väänänen (1967), 133. See in particular B. Löfstedt (1962).
[84] Cf. Calderini (1951), 252 f.
[85] On which see Gaeng (1968), 269; Pirson (1901), 50.
[86] Cf. Pighi (1964), 71. Nor is it true that *postae* (467.23) stands for *depostae* (as Calderini asserts). See below, v.12.

is well attested in vulgar texts.[87] The consonant cluster /ks/ was reduced to /s/,[88] and the initial vowel then lost.

Carnoy (1906, 111 f.) argued that aphaeresis in the Spanish inscriptions was a sandhi phenomenon, in that it tended to occur after words which ended with a vowel. B. Löfstedt (1961, 114) questions this explanation, and his doubts are reinforced by our example. Since *spectemus* occurs at the start of a sentence, it looks to be hypercorrective against prothesis rather than phonetically determined. If so it is evidence for the existence at this early date of prothesis. The first example of prothesis is at Pompeii,[89] but in the foreign place-name *Ismurna* (*CIL* IV.7221) before a non-Latin consonant cluster. As such it might have been aberrational. The example of *spectemus* in the letters (perhaps the earliest instance of aphaeresis?) suggests that it was not.

2 CONSONANTS

i Final /m/

One of the most striking features of the letters is the frequency with which final ⟨m⟩ is omitted.[90] In accusative singular endings it is omitted about once in every five instances (of 149 accusatives, including cases of participles, twenty-nine are written without ⟨-m⟩). When allowance is made for the conservatism of written forms of the language, it seems likely that by this time /-m/ had been lost in pronunciation. The evidence of the letters is in keeping with that of the Pompeian inscriptions.[91]

The examples of omission are as follows:

⟨-a⟩ for ⟨-am⟩

467.28 [un]a et uṇ[a] ṇigṛạ
467.30 aḍ Ḍ[el]ṭa
468.16 caueam gallinaria

[87] *TLL* v.2.1887.65 ff.; Grandgent (1907), 98.
[88] Cf. *destra* for *dextra*.
[89] Väänänen (1966), 48.
[90] Cf. Calderini (1951), 255 f.
[91] See Väänänen (1966), 71 ff.

468.27 ea q[u]am
468.33 bo̭[na]
468.49 Aphrodisia
468.51 scriba
468.59 collega
468.60 scriba
469.15 epistula

⟨-u⟩ for ⟨-um⟩

468.10 unu
468.10 unu
468.11 unu
468.11 unu
468.58 Seuerinu
468.59 Mar[c]ellu
469.19 f. caṛu
470.6 b[a]lteu̯
471.11 acu

⟨-e⟩ for ⟨-em⟩

467.28 co[lym]bade
468.33 re
468.52 centurione
468.56 Frontone
469.7 minoṛe
469.8 minore
469.17 minore
471.26 ad naue

⟨-am⟩ is written in full twenty-six times, ⟨-um⟩ (or ⟨-om⟩) seventy times (including seven cases in participles of various types) and ⟨-em⟩ twenty-four times. Thus ⟨-a⟩ is outnumbered only by about 2:1, ⟨-e⟩ by 3:1 and ⟨-u⟩ by more than 7:1. It is well established that in later texts of vulgar flavour ⟨-m⟩ is more often dropped in the first declension than in the other declensions.[92] Our letters might seem to show this tendency at a comparatively early period. But in fact it is the special

---

[92] See B. Löfstedt (1961), 227 ff., for evidence and an explanation of this phenomenon.

frequency of ⟨-um⟩ (as compared with ⟨-u⟩) rather than of ⟨-a⟩ (as compared with ⟨-am⟩) that is most striking. ⟨-a⟩ is scarcely more common proportionately than ⟨-e⟩. Similarly in the Pompeian inscriptions final ⟨-m⟩ is retained more often after ⟨u⟩ than in other environments.[93] This is a phenomenon which demands explanation.

According to Väänänen (1966, 76), in the first declension 'toute distinction entre cas sujet et cas régime était effacée après l'amuissement de -m, tandis que dans les thèmes en -o- cette distinction était nettement sentie, puisque l's final du nom . . . était stable'. This explanation fails to take account of the third declension. There too the nominative was clearly set apart from the accusative by the presence of /s/ and other consonants in final position. If ⟨-m⟩ were usually written in the second declension because the nominative and accusative were still felt to be distinct, so it ought to have been considerably more common in the third declension than in the first.

It is well established that at the level of orthography ⟨-m⟩ is omitted more often after ⟨u⟩ in the fourth declension than in the second. Hence examples of the type *uersu* = *uersum* are more common than *bonu* = *bonum*.[94] When final ⟨-m⟩ in a second declension word is omitted in late texts the final vowel tends to be rendered as ⟨o⟩ rather than ⟨u⟩. This distinction between the second and fourth declensions could not possibly have had any basis in pronunciation: it was purely graphemic. Since it was felt that the written form *uersu* existed but that *bonu* did not, *uersu* was admitted in writing as an accusative but *bonu* was largely avoided.[95] Herein lies the explanation of the frequency of ⟨-m⟩ in second declension accusatives.

If the change /u/ > /o̧/ had not fully taken place by this period (and we have argued that, unlike that of /i/ > /ȩ/, it is insecurely attested in the letters), a phonetic representation of the accusative singular of, say, *uir* would necessarily be *uiru*. But since such forms were felt to be anomalous in writing, they were avoided and the learned form retained. At

[93] Väänänen (1966), 76.   [94] B. Löfstedt (1961), 117 f.
[95] See B. Löfstedt (1961), 118.

a later period, when /u/ had definitely changed to /o̜/, accusatives in ⟨-o⟩ became very common. We thus have indirect evidence that in the early second century the change /u/ > /o̜/ was incomplete.

The following are the examples of omission of ⟨-m⟩ in words of other types:

468.12 aute
468.21 iacu̜[i]sse
468.22 speraba
469.20 sequndu
470.26 boleba
471.18 f. aute

ii Assimilation of final consonants: final /t/ and /d/
There are some clear cases of final consonants assimilated to what follows (or, in compounds, of the final consonant of the first element assimilated to the initial sound of the second element):[96]

468.9, 14 imboluclum = inuolucrum
468.26 im mensem
468.65 im perpetuo
469.7 imbenire
469.16 imuenerit
470.26 im bia (= uia)
471.19 imueni

At 471.32 (*im inpendia*) it seems that the final consonant of the preposition was labialised in anticipation of the expected *im-*, but that the writer then recomposed to *in-*. At 470.5 *anbo[bus* may be hypercorrective against the tendency for /n/ to be labialised before another labial. The spelling *con* (see II.1.i) indicates that constant assimilation of /m/ > /n/ before certain consonants led to a feeling that *con* was the original form of the word. See below, III.2.i, on *illan*.

But while most of the above examples are straightforward enough, final /t/ and /d/ raise considerable difficulties. The

[96] Cf. Calderini (1951), 256.

constant alternation between ⟨t⟩ and ⟨d⟩ in final position found from the late Republic onwards[97] suggests that the classic neutralisation of the opposition of voiceless /t/ and voiced /d/[98] had taken place in Latin,[99] at least in monosyllables and 'grammatical' words. But it is the form in which this neutralisation was realised which is open to question.

It is often the case that the 'unmarked' member of an opposition will occur in the position of neutralisation.[100] Thus when the opposition voiced *v.* voiceless of /d/ — /t/ is neutralised, only the voiceless /t/ may be found. So German has only /t/ in final position, whereas English still has the opposition /d/— /t/. It is apparently because of this general tendency that J. Safarewicz (1964, 99) states: 'On écrivait, il est vrai, *apud*, *illud*, *id*, *sed*, etc., mais on prononçait sans aucun doute une consonne sourde à la fin du mot, c.-à-d. la même consonne qui existait dans les mots *caput*, *it* "il marche", *amet* (subj.), *amat*, etc. La preuve en sont les fautes trouvées dans les inscriptions où on lit *aput* (*CIL* I².593.15), *it* "id" etc.: ces graphies fautives apparaissent à partir de la deuxième moitié du Ier siècle avant n.è.' But this assertion is not supported by the evidence. It is true that ⟨t⟩ is sometimes written for ⟨d⟩ in final position, but it is probably more common for ⟨d⟩ to be written for ⟨t⟩. So in the letters there are sixteen examples of ⟨d⟩ for ⟨t⟩, but only three of ⟨t⟩ for ⟨d⟩. Though devoicing of /d/ might cause apparently haphazard alternations of orthography between ⟨t⟩ and ⟨d⟩, such alternations are not in themselves sufficient proof of devoicing in all environments. Neutralisation can take various forms, all of which might be reflected in the orthography in the same or a similar way.[101] Only if false spellings showing ⟨t⟩ for ⟨d⟩ outnumbered those

---

[97] See, e.g., Sommer (1914), 274 f.; Grandgent (1907), 119; Väänänen (1966), 70, (1967), 63; B. Löfstedt (1961), 138. Cf. Quint. 1.7.5.

[98] On neutralisation, see Martinet (1968) [1973]; Robins (1971), 148 f.; Lyons (1971), 115 ff.

[99] For some types of neutralisation in Latin, see Anderson (1964–65).

[100] Lyons (1971), 126 f.

[101] On the various forms of neutralisation, see Martinet (1968) [1973], 76.

of the inverse kind decisively could we be sure that devoicing had occurred.

Neutralisation may also be manifested in assimilation of the phoneme to what follows.[102] So it is Väänänen's view (1966, 70) that /t/ tended to be retained (or /d/ devoiced) before a voiceless consonant, but voiced before a voiced consonant or vowel.[103] He explains the Pompeian examples *at quem* (*CIL* IV.1880) and *at porta* (*CIL* IV.2013) as due to assimilation of this type.[104] That this explanation is at least along the right lines is suggested by the treatment of the final consonant of the reflexes in early Romance of the monosyllables *ad*, *et*, *aut* and *quid*. A voiced consonant seems to have occurred before vowels, while before consonants there was either assimilation or loss of the final consonant.[105]

On the other hand if the Pompeian inscriptions are looked at as a whole, we do not find clear-cut evidence of the working of assimilation. Alongside the above examples note *CIL* IV.2400 *set intra* and *CIL* IV.1824 *quit ego*. Nor in the letters does it seem, at least at first sight, that voicing or devoicing is determined by what follows. The following are the examples of aberrational spellings:

467.24 quit mute[t]ur
468.2 ed domino
468.8 ed sequrum
468.21 ud contentus
468.22 f. ed itarum
468.25 ed udones
468.30 ed praeterea
468.42 ud continuo
468.43 ed [sci]as
468.43 f. ed inuentus
468.46 ed pater
468.47 ed fratres
468.50 f. ed Saturninum
470.19 ed pergerٍ[e

[102] Martinet (1968) [1973], *loc. cit.*
[103] Cf. Grandgent (1907), 119.
[104] Cf. Väänänen (1967), 63.
[105] Väänänen (1967), 72.

471.13 ed ibi
471.16 f. inquid, quod
471.22 f. reliquid con
472.10 aput te
472.17 [a]t te
5395.4 ed me
5395.5 ed iussus
5395.11 ed abes

Of the twenty-two examples, only ten could be said to exhibit assimilation of the type concerned. Confronted by such evidence, one is tempted to adopt another hypothesis. It is possible that the neutralisation was realised either by random variation between the two phonemes, or by a sound intermediate between them.[106] But though these possibilities might appear attractive, certain features of the above examples give us pause.

It will be seen that six of the examples which arguably show assimilation precede vowels (or semi-vowels), and another three precede either the voiced or voiceless dental (or alveolar) plosive. It is in these environments that the assimilation of /d/ > /t/ or /t/ > /d/ (a minimal change, involving only the state of the glottis; it is not as easily detected as assimilations — such as /n/ > /m/ — which involve a movement in the position of the articulators) is most easily apprehended. Before consonants other than /t/ and /d/, though assimilation of voice might occur, the resultant phoneme is not easily picked up by the untrained ear. Hence in these environments there is greater likelihood of inaccurate orthographic representation of the assimilation, especially in words of little stress (like the connective *et*). I conclude that neutralisation of the opposition /t/ — /d/ in final position usually (see further below) took the form of assimilation to what followed, but that this assimilation was not regularly apprehended in all environments.

It must be noted that it is almost exclusively in monosyllables and grammatical words that orthographic confusion is

[106] On which see Martinet (1968) [1973], 76.

apparent. In verb forms there was greater resistance to assimilation.

Inquid and *reliquid* may be treated as special cases. ⟨d⟩ is often found in final position in these words.[107] It is to be explained as due to orthographic contamination between *inquit* and *reliquit* on the one hand and *quid* on the other. Though B. Löfstedt (1961, 138 n. 2) rejects the view that the spelling *aput* was caused by contamination with *caput*, it cannot be denied that ⟨d⟩ is written for ⟨t⟩ particularly often in words to which there corresponds a similar word showing final ⟨-d⟩ rather than ⟨-t⟩ (cf. *at–ad*, *it–id*, *quot–quod*).[108]

At 471.19 the ⟨t⟩ of *post* is dropped before a following ⟨p⟩. Cf. Cic. *Orat*. 157 *et posmeridianas quadrigas quam postmeridianas quadriiugas lubentius dixerim*. *Pos* (the Romance form) is commonly attested in vulgar texts.[109] It should be noted that /t/ is not simply lost before a consonant, but between /s/ and a consonant. Final /t/ is not lost in other monosyllables (e.g. *et*, *at*) before consonants. The form *pos* must first have emerged before consonants as a result of the tendency for threefold consonant clusters to be reduced. It would then have been extended to other (pre-vocalic) environments.

In verb endings final /t/ is often lost completely both in early inscriptions and at Pompeii.[110] There is a comparable example at 471.34 (*uendedi*).

iii Final /s/

It has been seen that there is abundant evidence in the letters for the loss of final /m/. It is therefore the more noteworthy to find a paucity of evidence for the loss of final /s/. Despite the

---

[107] For examples see Seelmann (1885), 366; Carlton (1973), 149.

[108] For examples see Seelmann (1885), *loc. cit.*; Sommer (1914), 274 f.; Väänänen (1966), 70.

[109] See Neue and Wagener (1892–1905), II, 825; Pirson (1901), 104 f.; Sommer (1914), 299; Josephson (1950), 84; Väänänen (1966), 71; B. Löfstedt (1961), 134 f.

[110] See Väänänen (1966), 70 f., for examples. For a recent discussion of the question, see B. Löfstedt (1961), 135 f.

doubts of some scholars,[111] it is likely that /-s/ was successfully restored by the early Empire before being lost again in certain areas. In the letters there are just two examples of ⟨-s⟩ omitted, and one of these is a special case: 468.25 *subtalare ed udones*; 471.21 *pater meu sopera*. In the second example the omission occurs before /s/, a common enough occurrence in inscriptions also.[112] The other case may be due to scribal error, since there is no definite proof of the authenticity of the loss at this period.

iv Voicing of intervocalic stops

It is generally believed that the voicing of intervocalic stops is not unambiguously attested until about the fifth century (though doubts are expressed by some: see B. Löfstedt (1961), 140 f.). Campanile (1971, 58 ff.) has discussed the evidence for earlier sonorisation in the papyri, but his collection of examples is not complete. The papyri (and ostraca) now suggest that the process had begun in the early Empire or even before.

Väänänen (1966, 53) notes that many of the examples of possible sonorisation at Pompeii involve the graphemes ⟨c⟩ and ⟨g⟩. These examples must be omitted from consideration, for originally C had the value both of a voiced and voiceless stop. This early writing convention left its mark even on late epigraphy. Indeed, in Diehl's collection of vulgar inscriptions (1910), of some seventy examples of substitution of voiced-stop graphemes for voiceless or vice versa in all positions (I omit alternations between ⟨t⟩ and ⟨d⟩ in final position, and cases of recomposition after assimilation, such as 856 *scribtis*), fifty-five show the use of ⟨c⟩ for ⟨g⟩, and seven that of ⟨g⟩ for ⟨c⟩. Such misspellings rarely occur in the papyri.

---

[111] Notably B. Löfstedt (1961), 129 ff. On the whole question see the useful discussion by Hamp (1959).

[112] So at 468.41 (*si qui sibi*) *qui* is used instead of *quis* before /s/. On this tendency, see Löfstedt (1933–42), II, 82 f. For the omission of final ⟨s⟩ before another /s/ in inscriptions, see Carnoy (1906), 183; Väänänen (1966), 77.

Campanile does not observe that there is a case of intervocalic voicing in Terentianus (471.14 e⟨x⟩pediui = expetiui; cf. Sp., Pg. *pedir*, Log. *pedire*). Another notable omission is *dublices* on a first century ostracon from Tell Edfou (quoted by Cavenaile (1958), 292). /p/ shows the same development before /l/ as between vowels. Cf. Fr. *double* < *duplum*, Sp. *pueblo* < *poplus*, etc. A particularly early misspelling which probably belongs here is the apparent hyperurbanism *detuci* = *deduci* (Cavenaile (1958), 103, dated to the period 40–37 B.C.). Cf. *audem* (Cavenaile (1958), 237 II.5, from the Neronian period), *galliga* (Cavenaile (1958), 114, A.D. 130), *pecado*, *peccadis* (Cavenaile (1958), 45, prior to A.D. 115; cf. Sp., Pg. *pecado*, Log. *pekkadu*).

Some of these examples are remarkably early, and difficult to explain away. I interpret them as almost conclusive evidence that sonorisation had begun early. Moreover their provenance establishes once and for all that Latin sonorisation had nothing to do with substrate (Celtic) influence.

v   /b/ and /w/

It is probable that at a relatively early period /b/ and /w/ both changed quality, becoming a bilabial fricative ([β]) of the type now represented by Sp. intervocalic ⟨b⟩ and ⟨v⟩.[113] Hence there are fluctuations of orthography in inscriptions and texts because neither letter adequately rendered the new phoneme. It is usually the grapheme ⟨b⟩ that is preferred, though that is not likely to be of phonetic significance.[114] Since ⟨u⟩ already had a vocalic value, it was not favoured. In the letters ⟨b⟩ for ⟨u⟩ is more numerous than ⟨u⟩ for ⟨b⟩: 467.16 *iui*, 468.9, 14 *imboluclum*, 468.12 *pulbin[o]*, 469.6 *qumqupibit*, 469.7 *imbenire*, 469.8 *bolt*, 470.8 *benio*, 470.20 *ben[i]ant*, 470.24 *beni*, 470.26 *boleba*, 470.26 *bia*, 471.32 *negabit*, 471.13 *ibi*, 5395.11 *imboluclum*.[115]

The confusion is found mainly in initial position. There are

---

[113] Väänänen (1966), 50 ff., (1967), 51 f.; B. Löfstedt (1961), 149 ff.; Carlton (1973), 119 ff.

[114] B. Löfstedt (1961), 153 f.   [115] Cf. Calderini (1951), 256 f.

two definite examples in intervocalic position and another two which are probable. In the Romania the falling together of /b/ and /w/ is chiefly apparent intervocally, though there are areas in which it is total or almost total.[116] In early Vulgar Latin the merger must have taken place in all positions, before the restoration of a distinction in some areas in initial position and after liquids.[117] Certainly in two of our earliest sources for Vulgar Latin (the letters and the Pompeian inscriptions) the confusion is more noticeable at the start of words. Indeed, in the latter there is no sure example of ⟨b⟩ for ⟨u⟩ or ⟨u⟩ for ⟨b⟩ in intervocalic position.[118]

vi ⟨q⟩, ⟨k⟩

Throughout the letters ⟨q⟩ instead of ⟨c⟩ is constantly written before ⟨u⟩:[119] 468.8 *sequrum*, 469.6 *qumqupibit*, 20 *sequrum*, 470.22 *sequrus*, 471.25 *tequm*, 29 *qurauit*, 31 *pauqum*, 472.5 *mequm*. This orthography is an old one (there are examples such as *qura*, *pequnia* and *oqupare* in inscriptions of the Gracchan period),[120] which might appear to reflect the fact that /k/ has various allophones determined by the quality of the following vowel. The Latin alphabet possessed three graphemes (⟨c⟩, ⟨k⟩, ⟨q⟩) which could be employed to render /k/. The grammarians laid down a rule that ⟨k⟩ should be written before ⟨a⟩, and ⟨q⟩ before ⟨u⟩:[121] Donat. *GL* IV.368.7 ff. *qui nesciunt, quotiens a sequitur, k litteram praeponendam esse, non c; quotiens u sequitur, per q, non per c scribendum* (cf. Vel. Long. *GL* VII.53.14).[122] The influence of this rule is further reflected in the letters by the use of ⟨k⟩ a few times before ⟨a⟩: 467.1 *karissimo* (in connection with which note Velius Longus' remarks, *loc. cit.*), 14 *kasus*, 18 *karum*.

Despite appearances, the grammarians do not genuinely seem to have recognised allophones of /k/. It is more likely

---

[116] See, e.g., Politzer (1952). [117] Cf. B. Löfstedt (1961), 153 ff.
[118] Väänänen (1966), 51.   [119] Cf. Calderini (1951), 253 f.
[120] See Lindsay (1894), 7. Cf. Coleman (1963), 17.
[121] See Kent (1945), 52 f.
[122] See further Coleman (1963), *loc. cit.*

that the above rule sprang from a desire to eliminate redundancy in the alphabet by giving a function to each of the graphemes. Redundancy and inadequacy in the alphabet exercised the grammarians considerably.

The most appropriate position for ⟨q⟩ was obviously before ⟨u⟩. Since [kʷ] (represented usually by ⟨qu⟩) lost its labial element before /u/ (e.g. *antiquus* > It. *antico*), ⟨q⟩ could be used in this environment to render a non-labialised stop, if ⟨u⟩, which might be interpreted as a sign of lip-rounding, was omitted.[123]

vii ⟨tl⟩

At 469.12 the syncopated form of *situlas* is written as *sitlas*, though as a rule the cluster /tl/ was not tolerated in Latin of any period. Hence the I.-E. nominal suffix *-tl* appears as *-cl*:[124] e.g. *poclum* < *potlum*. Another early example of the change is seen in the loan-word *anclare* < ἀντλεῖν. It is a modification which is general in Italic (cf. Osc. *puklum*).[125]

Numerous examples are found in later Latin. In the *Appendix Probi* there occur the three items *uetulus non ueclus* (5), *uitulus non uiclus* (6), and *capitulum non capiclum* (167). According to *CGL* v.248.14 *fistula uulgo fiscla dicitur*, and in reference to *astula* Cassiodorus states (*GL* vii.205.7) *in elisione ascla*. *Mencla* is attested for *mentula* (*CGL* ii.481.40), and is reflected in Romance (e.g. It. *minchia*).[126] *Ustulare* survives as Prov. *usclar*.[127] Note too the hypercorrect spellings *Artlaus* = *Archelaus* (Diehl (1910), 481) and *Astlas* = *Asclas* (*CIL* vi.647).

But examples of ⟨tl⟩ are not lacking. In the Pompeian inscriptions there is alternation between *mentula* and *mentla*,

---

[123] For similar spellings at Pompeii, see Väänänen (1966), 53 n. 1.
[124] See Buck (1933), 148, 329.
[125] Buck (1933), 329.
[126] Meyer-Lübke (1935), 5513. On *menclilingia*, see *TLL* viii.695.60 and Heraeus (1925), 317 n. 1.
[127] Väänänen (1967), 68; cf. Grandgent (1907), 120.

but *mencla* does not occur (*mentula CIL* IV.1441, 1776, 1830, 1882, 1938, 2400; *mentla* 760.2, 1391, 3103, 4246; cf. *CIL* III.10189.16, VII.204). *Crustlum* is found at *CIL* X.333 and XI.3303, though it is *crusclum* that survives.[128] *Vitlus* occurs at *CIL* V.2460 and *uitlina* at *CGL* III.364.5. Schuchardt (1866–68, II, 405, 429, 431) quotes examples of *capitlares*, *fistlator*, *crustlum* and *titlum* (but it is *ticlum* which shows reflexes in Romance).[129]

During the period of transition between an original form with a termination -*tulum* or the like and the syncopated form containing the cluster /kl/, at the time when the learned form was still conceived as -*tulum* a word might be written, though not pronounced, with the cluster ⟨tl⟩ as a compromise between the spoken and learned forms. Hence there are sporadic examples of an anomalous cluster. But it should not be assumed on the basis of the written language that this cluster had any place in the spoken registers.

It is *sicla* that survives in Italian (*secchia*).[130] But it is possible that as a bilingual Terentianus was tolerant of the consonant cluster /tl/. This possibility is made more likely by the presence of the Latin loan word σίτλιον in a Greek papyrus (*P. Oxy.* 1290). σίκλα, however, lives on in NGr.

viii Assimilation involving /r/ and /l/

I quote the examples of this phenomenon without comment: 468.9, 14, 5395.11 *imboluclum* = *inuolucrum*,[131] 468.11 *gla*[*b*]*a*⟨*tu*⟩*lum* = *grabatulum*.

ix Aspiration

There would be no point in quoting the various examples of the omission of the aspirate both in initial position and inter-

---

[128] Meyer-Lübke (1935), 2347.
[129] Meyer-Lübke (1935), 8761. See further Battisti (1949), 114; Diehl (1910), 310–14.
[130] Meyer-Lübke (1935), 7962.
[131] Omitted by Calderini (1951), 255.

vocally (notably in *mi*).¹³² Usually the Greek aspirated plosives are represented in the learned manner by means of digraphs (e.g. 467.27, 28, 468.17, 18, 19).

x Gemination

There is an almost total lack of examples of false gemination or simplification. But *T]urranium* at 468.54 shows the inverse tendency to the 'law of *mamilla*' (i.e. *mamma*, but *mamilla*).¹³³ The pattern single consonant + stressed vowel + geminate is the norm in Latin (cf. *sacellus* alongside *saccus*). The scribe seems to have been hesitant about making a foreign word (*Turannium*) comply with a Latin tendency. Hence he falsely doubled the pre-tonic consonant and simplified the post-tonic.

[132] Examples are given by Calderini (1951), *loc. cit.*
[133] See Väänänen (1966), 60 f.; B. Löfstedt (1961), 167 f.

III MORPHOLOGY AND SYNTAX

1 CASE, PREPOSITIONS AND THE NOMINAL SYSTEM

i Case with prepositions

Evidence for the generalisation of the accusative as the prepositional case is insecurely based on examples which show an accusative singular with a preposition, for final ⟨-m⟩ was liable to be added haphazardly as well as omitted: note 471.27 *tam magna lites factam est*; cf. Cavenaile (1958), 303 *scito enim me uxorem ducerem* (= *ducere*). However, the letters contain an unambiguous example of *con* with a plural accusative: 471.22 *con tirones*. The presence of this expression makes it likely that the various instances of what appear to be singular accusatives with *con* are genuine: 468.12 *con culcitam*, 470.10 *con fratrem*, 471.23 *con matrem*. *In*, *pro* and perhaps *de* are also so used: 468.14 (cf. 5395.11) *abes in imboluclum*, 26 *bis . . . im mensem*, 471.29 *pro xylesphongium*. Cf. 468.32 [*resc*]*rib*[*as de*] *salutem*.

The use of *sopera* too at 471.21 may exhibit the same tendency: *litem abuit Ptolemes pater meu sopera vestimenta mea*. *Super* + abl. is common enough in the sense *de* + abl., but *super* does not normally govern the accusative when it has this function. Souter (1949, *s.v.*) quotes the usage from Tertullian, and this passage should probably be added.

The inconsistency of case seen at 467.16 *me probaui in militia* and 467.22 *me pr*[*o*]*barem in militiam* must be due to the indeterminacy of the action of the verb between static and directional. Inconsistencies of this type occur at all periods.

It is of particular note that there are almost no inverse examples of the ablative used with prepositions instead of the accusative.[1] We are given an unobscured glimpse of the language in a state of flux: for once it is unnecessary to make allowance for the hypercorrective tendencies usually found in vulgar texts. The new system, in which the function of prepositional expressions is carried by the preposition alone (with the accusative serving as the prepositional case), stands side by side with the old system, in which there are variations of case, for the most part redundant, with prepositions. At 468.12 (*emeram aute illuc con culcitam et pulbin[o]*) *con* may be used with both the accusative and ablative, if the restoration is correct.[2]

In classical Latin it is chiefly with *in* that the ablative is functional, since it distinguishes the static use of the preposition from the directional. But in Vulgar Latin the distinction between static and directional adverbials was not formally marked (see below). Hence the need for an accusative–ablative opposition in prepositional expressions was removed.

ii Local and directional expressions

A number of times a static complement is used with a verb of motion in the typical vulgar manner.[3] The redundancy of classical expressions such as *huc uenerunt* (in which direction is marked by both the adverb and verb) was eliminated in Vulgar Latin by the employment of non-directional complements.

At 472.10 f. *apud* is found with *uenio*: *spero me celerius aput te uenturum*. This is a usage which is censured by the grammarians: Don. *GL* iv.393.23 (*soloecismus est*) '*apud amicum eo*' pro '*ad amicum*'; Cled. *GL* v.77.2 f. *apud tantum in loco significat, ut 'apud amicum sum', nec possumus dicere*

---

[1] But *im perpetuo* (468.65) may be of this type. According to the editors the usual expressions are *perpetuo* and *in perpetuum*.

[2] If *pulbino* is right, it could hardly be interpreted as an accusative with the ⟨-m⟩ lost. There is no other example in the letters of ⟨-o⟩ (representing /o/) functioning as an accusative.

[3] On the use of *ubi = quo*, etc., see Hofmann and Szantyr (1965), 277.

'*apud amicum uado*'. Most of the examples of the usage quoted at *TLL* II.344.34 ff. are in late or vulgar texts, but there are also isolated instances of indifference to the above distinction in Sallust and Tacitus.

The use of the locative *Alexandrie* as a directional (as well as locative) complement is exactly parallel in type to the above expression: e.g. 471.25 *uen[i]o tequm Alexandrie*; 31 f. *ut possim uenire con rebus meis Alexandrie*; 33 *ueni, dicet, Alexandrie* (cf. 470.19, 471.15, 35, 472.9). The same usage is found in Petronius (62.1).[4] So in the Greek letters at 477.15 the original stative ἐν + dat. may be employed as a directional:[5] γενοῦ ἐν] 'Αλ[εξ]ανδρείᾳ.

The habitual use of a locative as a dual-purpose complement was the first stage in the fossilising of the locative as the place name itself.[6]

At 469.19 *domu* is accompanied by the preposition *a*, in a context which is unfortunately incomplete. Though we cannot tell whether *domu* was qualified, it would not be discordant with this type of Latin if it were not. As a rule in classical Latin *domo* (or *domu*) is used without a preposition unless it is qualified in some way (see Cled. *GL* v.25.15 '*ab domo*' *non dicimus nisi pronomen addamus:* '*a domo mea*' *vel* '*a domo tua*'). Its semi-adverbial character prevented it taking an adjective.[7] But the process of encroachment by prepositional expressions on independent case usage was taking place throughout the history of Latin. The fossilised forms of *domus*, etc., were not lacking in prepositional alternatives even in early Latin. *Ab domo* is found in Plautus: *Aul*. 105 *ab domo abeundumst mihi*; *Epid*. 681 *num ab domo apsum* (for a similar context in which the preposition is omitted, see *Cas*. 484).

At 468.47 *domo* is used with locative function: *et scias*

---

[4] See Hofmann and Szantyr (1965), 150.
[5] On which usage, see Moulton (1908), 245.
[6] On which tendency, see Hofmann and Szantyr (1965), 151; Grandgent (1907), 42 f.; Consentius, *GL* v.349.4.
[7] See Ernout and Thomas (1953), 108.

domo perb[e]ne omnia recte esse. The first declension locative in *-ae* remained in constant use until very late because of the frequency of *Romae*, which served as the analogy for the use of the morph in other first declension words. But in the second declension *-i* was not supported by the existence of a similarly frequent word.[8] In this declension the locative was replaced partly by prepositional expressions, but also by the locatival use of the ablative. For the use of *domo* as an equivalent of the more learned *domi*, see *TLL* v.1.1962.29 ff.; cf. 1977.38 f.[9] The usage is especially common in inscriptions of vulgar flavour, but it is not unknown in classical authors. However, in the latter it can often be interpreted as instrumental (*TLL* v.1.1962.31).

Of particular note is 467.26 *scias domọ nostrae deorum beneficio omnia recte esse*, where *domo* is not qualified by *nostra* but by *nostrae*. The lack of grammatical concord underlines the vitality of the *-ae* locative morph. In the eyes of the writer *domo* was locatival and also feminine. Its adjectival complement was thus a feminine locative in *-ae*.

At 468.34 (*de uiç[e] iṇ do⟨mó⟩*) it is possible that *in domo* is used as another alternative to *domi*, but the text is uncertain. In classical Latin this expression is usually only substituted for *domi* when *domi* would have to be qualified, or in oppositions with other prepositional expressions (*TLL* v.1.1963.55 ff., 1964.10. ff., 1968.13 ff.), but there are sporadic examples which can only be put down to the constant encroachment of prepositions on the independent inflections. Petronius uses *in domo* in this way in the *Cena* (43.8, 57.10).

iii   quo tempus *(471.17)*

It might be thought that *tempus* (*quo tempus autem ueni omnia praefuerunt*) is an unconstrued nominative,[10] but a glance at the examples of this construction shows that *quo tempus* does not fit the predominating patterns. There are two

---

[8] See Löfstedt (1933–42), II, 74 ff.
[9] Cf. Hofmann and Szantyr (1965), 145.
[10] On which construction see Hofmann and Szantyr (1965), 28.

types of unconstrued nominative found in adjective–noun combinations. In the first place the first element of a habitual combination may be left uninflected (e.g. *olusatri*).[11] But in our expression it is the second element which is not inflected. Secondly, an attributive adjective in a common expression may be uninflected (e.g. *uini uetus*).[12] Again *quo tempus* fails to fit the pattern, for it is the substantival component which is uninflected.[13]

In late Latin the accusative *tempus* was fossilised as an indicator of point of time.[14] It would seem that *quo tempus* is a conflation of two different types of temporal expression: *quo tempore* + *tempus*. Since *tempus* could express point of time, it could be left in that form to stand alongside *quo*.

The presence of this construction in the letters implies that *tempus* had already been fossilised as a temporal accusative in Vulgar Latin, though it has usually been thought that the usage belongs to late Latin.[15]

iv Accusative of price

At 469.17 there is what looks like an accusative of price: *ęrgo [m]ęrca minore pretium*. The editors appear to regard *minore* as an ablative and *pretium* as an unconstrued nominative.[16] But we have seen above that the existence of such unconstrued nominatives is uncertain. Nor on the other hand would it be convincing to treat the expression as ablatival, with final ⟨-m⟩ hypercorrectively added to the second member (as in *factam*, 471.27). ⟨-m⟩ is far more often lost than added in the letters, and it is very simple to suppose that the ⟨-m⟩ of *minore*

---

[11] See Hofmann and Szantyr (1965), *loc. cit.*; Uddholm (1953), 95 f.

[12] See Hofmann and Szantyr (1965), *loc. cit.*

[13] The editors (on 469.7) quote an example of the expression *de suo prop⟨r⟩ium = de suo proprio*, but *proprium* need not be an unconstrued nominative. For a preposition originally taking the ablative used inconsistently with both accusative and ablative, see Diehl (1910), 1267 *ex equtibus siculares*.

[14] See Hofmann and Szantyr (1965), 42; and especially Norberg (1943), 36. Numerous accusatives are so fossilised in late Latin.

[15] See Norberg (1943), *loc. cit.*

[16] It is pointless to compare lines 7 and 8, where *minore* occurs, for in both places the termination of *pretium* is missing.

MORPHOLOGY AND SYNTAX 41

has been dropped.[17] It is true that if the terminations ⟨-o⟩ and ⟨-um⟩ were in alternation as accusatives, then by analogy ⟨-um⟩ might be falsely written for ⟨-o⟩ in the ablative. But we have already seen that the accusative termination ⟨-o⟩ does not occur in the letters: hence we should not expect a hypercorrect ablative in ⟨-um⟩. Moreover the accusative of price occurs for the first time as early as the *Cena Trimalchionis*: 43.4 *uendidit enim uinum, quantum ipse uoluit*. If we can regard our example as such, it must occupy an important place in the evidence concerning the development of the construction.

The fundamental discussion of the usage is by Löfstedt (1936, 170 ff.). Löfstedt was followed by Norberg (1943, 103 ff.), who added some new examples but did not question or modify Löfstedt's explanation. Löfstedt (1936, 173) pointed out that many examples of the construction contain not a noun in the accusative, but a pronominal or adjectival neuter: it was only in later Latin that substantives started to appear.[18] Löfstedt saw these neuters, which could readily be fossilised as adverbial accusatives, as the starting point of the usage.

But the letters of Terentianus at a relatively early date seem to contain a substantival example. Nor is there any reason why they should not. The accusative of price is nothing other than one variety of the accusative of extension. An example such as ours is parallel to other varieties such as that of distance (Livy 30.29.2 *Zama quinque dierum iter a Carthagine abest*), of dimension (Caes. *Gall.* 7.24.1 *aggerem latum pedes trecentos triginta*), of degree (Ter. *Phorm.* 247 *incredibilest quantum erum ante eo sapientia*), or of measure (Varro *Ling.* 5.173 *denarii, quod denos (nummos) aeris ualebant*).[19] This type of accusative marks the extent of space, time, or weight occupied by an object or action. It was a

---

[17] Indeed at 1.7 *minore pr[etium]* might be accusative (*uide si potes imbenire minore pr[etium]*), though the editors take it as an ablative.
[18] So Norberg (1943), 103; Hofmann and Szantyr (1965), 73; Väänänen (1967), 118.
[19] See Ernout and Thomas (1953), 30 ff., for these examples.

simple step for it to express measure of value (note the example quoted above from Varro) or price.[20] Löfstedt's factor may have been one of the determinants of the construction, but the structural conditions of the language were such as to accommodate it readily. If a substantival accusative could be used to mark value, so too could it be used to mark price.

v adiuto + *dat.* *(468.41, 471.28)*

The dative with *adiuto* finds a parallel in the *Cena Trimalchionis*: 62.11 *nobis adiutasses*. It was the analogy of expressions such as *adesse*, *succurro* and *auxilium ferre* + dat. which produced the usage.[21]

vi Ablative of time

Twice the ablative is used in the manner typical of vulgar texts to express duration of time: 467.36 *bene ualere te opto multis annis* (cf. 468.64).[22]

vii Partitive apposition

Terentianus makes constant use of this construction (which is found mainly in colloquial writings from an early date onwards)[23] in 468: e.g. 10 f. *habes amicla par unu amictoria [pa]r unu sabana par unu saccos par unu gla[b]a⟨tu⟩lum* (cf. 17 ff., 25, 5395.3).

viii lites *(471.27)*

The editors (followed by Calderini (1951), 257; but cf. Pighi (1964), 71) state without explanation that this is an example of a plural for singular: *tam magna lites factam est*. But it is obviously a case of the remodelling of an imparisyllabic third declension noun so that the nominative has the same syllabic

---

[20] See Ernout and Thomas (1953), 32.

[21] For the use of the dative in vulgar texts with a wide range of verbs normally taking the accusative, see Hofmann and Szantyr (1965), 89; Löfstedt (1911), 151 f.; Norberg (1943), 146 ff.

[22] On this usage, see, e.g., Hofmann and Szantyr (1965), 148.

[23] See, e.g., Hofmann and Szantyr (1965), 44, 57.

structure as the oblique cases. For this tendency censured in the *Appendix Probi*, see 21 *pecten non pectinis*, 115 *glis non gliris*, 128 *grus non gruis*.

ix uitriae *(468.16)*

The editors restore as follows: *et accipias caueam gallinaria⟨m⟩ in qua ha[bes] sunthe[seis] uitriae et phialas quinarias . . . et calices paria sex et chartas . . .* The apparent nominative form *uitriae* requires explanation. According to the editors it is a case of 'nom. for acc., because its noun . . . is in form either nom. or acc.'. Pighi prefers to read *habet* in the sense *il y a*, but this does nothing to solve the problem, for this usage in Latin texts (attested first in the *H.A.*) is habitually accompanied by an accusative.[24] There is no doubt that the original restoration is right. Cf. in the same letter 9 f. *in quo habes amicla*, 14 *et abes . . . amictorium*, and 5395.11 *ed abes . . . amictori[u]m*.

Here indeed an unconstrued nominative would be tolerable. *Vitriae* is both an attributive adjective and it follows the noun (cf. the type *uini uetus*, above, III.1.iii). But there is another possibility which cannot be eliminated. The neuter plural substantive *uitrea* may have passed into the feminine first declension. *Vitriae* would then be a genitive of material identical to *ligni* (11) and *cori* (24) in the same letter. A singular substantive of this type with the sense 'glass' would be plausible. Indeed a singular *uitrium* with this sense is demanded by Romance (masculine) reflexes such as Sp. *vidrio*, Pg. *vidro*.[25]

x Gender

At 468.10 ff. the text runs as follows: *habes . . . gla[b]a⟨tu⟩lum ligni. emeram aute illuc . . .* Pighi (1964), 47 f. states that *illuc* could be masculine or neuter, but in fact it can be treated only as neuter (= *illud + ce*).[26] *Glabatulum*[27] must

---

[24] See, e.g., Löfstedt (1911), 43 f.   [25] Meyer-Lübke (1935), 9402.
[26] See Sommer (1914), 430; Neue and Wagener (1892–1905), II, 429.
[27] From *grabatulum* by assimilation. Cf. *imboluclum* = *inuolucrum* (see

therefore be a neuter. Cf. *GL* v.573.19 *nunc grabattum generis neutri*. So there are fluctuations between *lectus* and *lectum*.

In accordance with what has been said above (III.1.iv), *pretium* at 469.17 (and perhaps also at 469.7) must be masculine (cf. It. *prezzo*).

For the use of *hunc* = *hoc* at 468.15 (*abes . . . amictorium singlare, hunc tibi mater mea misit*), see Väänänen (1965), 34.

2   PRONOUNS

i   Demonstratives

In the *Cena Trimalchionis is* is very rare but *ille* occurs constantly.[28] But in most other texts traditionally described as vulgar (Anthimus is a notable exception), even those from a very much later period, *is* continues to be preferred.[29] Until the discovery of the letters of Terentianus it was difficult to decide whether the frequency of *is* in late texts was due to the conservatism of writing or to the continued survival of the word in popular speech (in other than monosyllabic forms: it is rare in all types of Latin from the late Republic onwards as a monosyllable). It now seems likely that *is* had been largely replaced by *ille* in all forms by the end of the first century. In the letters *ille* occurs thirty-one times (five times reinforced by the particle *-ce*), but *is* only four times, always in polysyllabic forms (467.16 *per eọs*, 467.29 *ex e*[*i*]*s*, 468.27 *ea*, 472.8 *eum*). *Iste* occurs twice, both times arguably with second person reference in the classical manner: 467.28 *amphorae istae sunt pares ill*[*is*]; 468.21 *rogo te . . . ud contentus sis ista*. There are three examples of *hic* (467.29, 468.15, 471.16), the third of which is in the expression *hoc est*. The editors also restore *is* twice at 467.9 (an unlikely restoration, in view of the above statistics), and *hic* at 467.14.

above, II.2.viii). It is safer to accept the editors' restoration than Pighi's *glabalum*. He states (1964, 47) that *glabalum* 'può essere grafia errata per *grabatum*, grafia semi-fonetica per *grabaclum, deformazione o abbreviazione del *sermo castrensis*.' I cannot believe this explanation.

[28] Stefenelli (1962), 37.   [29] B. Löfstedt (1961), 258 f.

It is misleading to state (so Calderini (1951), 258) that *illec* (= *illaec*) at 469.18 is due to the analogy of *haec*, as if it were an isolated aberration. The reinforced demonstratives *illaec*, *illic*, *illuc* had been in use since early Latin, as a glance at the *TLL* would have shown (VII.1.370.10 ff.). There is no need to suppose that *haec* was primary and *illaec* a later formation. Since *illaec* is ancient, both undoubtedly had the same origin. *Haec* consists of root **ha-*, followed by two separate particles, $\bar{i} + ce$,[30] and *illaec* had the same structure.

Illic (*illaec*, etc.) occurs some 200 times in Plautus and fifteen times in Terence, and it is also found elsewhere in early Latin (*TLL* VII.1.370.29 ff.). Later it is rare. However, its occurrence in both the Pompeian inscriptions[31] and now our letters (cf. Catull. 50.5) suggests that it was one of the many usages which long survived at a sub-literate level, though no longer in use in the literature. *Istic* had a similar history. It is common in comedy, but at a later period it turns up only sporadically, and then usually in writers of colloquial flavour (Catull.67.15, *CIL* IV.8617; *TLL* VII.1.495 f.).

The other examples of demonstratives with *-ce* are as follows: 468.12 *emeram aute illuc*; 469.6 *qumqupibit illuc*; 470.8 *a]ssequor illunc̣ et benio ad illunc*.

The final consonant of *illan* (468.28) (preceding *mi*) may be hypercorrective against the tendency for /n/ to be labialised before another labial (cf. *anbo[bus* at 470.5; see above, II.2.ii). Alternatively it may be due to the influence of the spelling of the reinforced forms of the accusative singular (cf. *illunc*). Or it could be a Grecising spelling (cf. 468.62 *nostrous*, and in particular the accusative *Isituchen* at 468.49).[32]

In 469 *illei* is five times written as the dative singular of the demonstrative (4, 8, 13, 14, 18). Since the same letter contains *reṣc̣reibae* (11), in which ⟨ei⟩ is used to render /ī/, it is possible that *illei* stands for *illi*.[33] But it is particularly striking

---

[30] Ernout (1953), 124.   [31] Väänänen (1966), 86.
[32] *Illan* is attested elsewhere: *TLL* VII.1.340.51.
[33] Calderini's suggestion (1951, 258) that the spelling may be a Grecism

that all five cases of *illei* are feminine. When the referent is masculine, *illi* is habitually used (e.g. 471.10, 22, 27 f., 31). *Illei* must stand for *illaei*, with the monophthongisation of the diphthong represented. *Illei* survives in Romance (It. *lei*).[34]

The masculine *illi* was remodelled to *illui*, probably on the analogy of *cui*.[35] It has usually been thought that *illaei* was a remodelling of the feminine dative *illae* (attested from early Latin onwards)[36] brought about under the influence of the rhythm of the masculine *illui*.[37] According to Grandgent (1907, 164) *illui* is found from the sixth century onwards. Whether or not this is true, it does not occur in the letters. Since *illei* does, the traditional explanation of the form should be abandoned.

It is difficult to believe that *illaei* shows a freak contaminated inflection (*illae* + *illi*)[38] fitting into no system. In fact the genitive and dative singulars of both the masculine and feminine each seem to have been restructured systematically. On the analogy of the relative–interrogative form a masculine genitive *illuius* emerged,[39] to which corresponded the new dative *illui*. The need felt for a distinctive feminine genitive caused *illīus* to be modified to *illaeius*. It would appear that since /ī/ in a masculine inflection often corresponded to /ae/ in a feminine (gen. sing. *boni–bonae*, nom. plur. *boni–bonae*, *qui–quae*, *hi–hae*, *illi–illae*, *ei–eae*), the /ī/ of *illius* was replaced to give a feminine form. In the pronominal declension the genitive singular termination always showed the graphemic sequence ⟨ius⟩, with the first grapheme representing either [ī] or more often [j] (or [jj]) (*eius*, *cuius*, *huius*). Hence the simple substitution of /ae/ for /ī/ would not have produced a recognisable genitive form. The obvious solution was to

---

can be rejected. ⟨ei⟩ spellings reflect an awareness that original /ei/ had fallen together with /ī/. See above, II.1.ii.

[34] See Elcock (1960), 80.
[35] Elcock (1965), *loc. cit.*, Grandgent (1907), 163 f.
[36] See Monteil (1974), 235.
[37] Elcock (1965), *loc. cit.*, Grandgent (1907), *loc. cit.*
[38] This appears to be Väänänen's view (1967, 130).
[39] Grandgent (1907), 164.

attach *-ius* (in which ⟨i⟩ represents [j] or [jj]) to *ae*. The result was a feminine genitive with the same trisyllabic structure as the masculine, and the same termination as most of the pronominal genitives.

That the sequence of events described here is correct is suggested by the existence of the form *illeus* in a British *defixio* cited by Collingwood and Wright (1965) (No. 7): *Tretia Maria defico et illeus vita*. This form shows the substitution of /ae/ (/ę/, or perhaps /ę̄/, rendered by ⟨e⟩) for /ī/. Subsequently the termination would have been felt to be anomalous and remodelled.

On the analogy of the new genitive a new dative *illaei* could be created: the genitive termination *-ius* was replaced by the dative *-ī*.

If the above explanation is accepted, the feminine forms must necessarily have been remodelled before the masculine: *illaeius* had as its starting point the original form *illius* rather than *illuius*. It is just such a relative chronology that is required to explain the situation in the letters, where the feminine dative has been remodelled but not the masculine.

Illim (471.24 *illim aḅit*[*u*]*ri*) can be mentioned here, though it is not a pronoun. The more usual classical form is *illinc*.[40] *Illim* is common in old Latin and also in Cicero's letters (*TLL* VII.1.380.7 ff.). It undoubtedly survived as a sub-literate colloquialism.

ii quis, qui

There is no sign of contamination of *quis* and *qui*[41] except at 468.41 *nesi si qui sibi aiutaueret*. But this is a special case, for the following consonant is /s/. We might compare the dropping of final ⟨s⟩ when there is an /s/ following (see above, II.2.iii).

iii nullus

At 467.13 (*nullus* [*co*]*ṃputauit kasus sụ*[*ae*] *u*[*itae*]) it seems

---

[40] On adverbs of this type, see Monteil (1974), 239.
[41] On these words, see Hofmann and Szantyr (1965), 554.

that *nullus* is used for *nemo*, though there is a gap near by in the text. A substantival use of *nullus* is plausible, for in Vulgar Latin *nemo* was displaced by *nullus* in all forms under the Empire.[42]

3 THE VERB

i Future

There are numerous synthetic futures in the letters (for *-b* futures, see 468.24, 471.10, 33; for those of the other type, see 467.6, 10, 25, 469.16, 470.17, 22, 24). Though there is an example in the Greek letters of the future periphrasis ἔχω + infin. (476.12 τοὔνπαλιν οὐκ ἔχεις ἀπ' ἐμοῦ ἀκ[οῦ]σαι) and another of μέλλω + infin. (477.42 f.), in the Latin *habeo* + infin. does not make an appearance. Yet, as we have seen, the phonological developments which were undermining the future are already in evidence. Oppositions such as *dicēs–dicis* and *delebit–deleuit* must have been obliterated in speech as a result of the falling together of /ē/ and /i/ and of /b/ and /w/. Clearly the transition from a synthetic to a periphrastic future system must have followed the above phonological changes. The theory of Jungemann (1955, 310 ff.)[43] that it was syntactic and morphological change which rendered certain vowel oppositions redundant does not, in the case of the future at least, square with the relative chronology of the restructuring of the vowel and consonant systems on the one hand, and the morpho-syntactic changes on the other. There must have been some time lag between the phonological changes and the full adoption of periphrastic futures.

At 471.32 f. (*negabit se abiturum*) there is a striking illustration of the way in which the merger of /b/ and /w/ was disturbing verb morphology. As the editors point out, the sense of the passage (= 'he denied that he had any') logically demands a present infinitive (*habere*). *Abiturum* has been substituted for *habere* under the influence of *negabit*, which

[42] Hofmann and Szantyr (1965), 204 f.
[43] See Spence (1965), 15, for criticism of this view.

has been falsely interpreted as a future. It appears that the scribe first took down the main verb with ⟨b⟩ representing [β], later interpreted the ⟨b⟩ as standing for original [b], and then mechanically changed *habere* to *abiturum* without considering the context. He might alternatively have been copying out Terentianus' own writing. In any case the lack of distinction between the future and perfect, and the confusion which it might cause, is obvious.

A few alternatives to the synthetic future are in evidence. At 467.23 we find *missurus es* (followed a few lines later at 25 by *scr[i]bes*, which is identical in function), and at 472.14 f. *daturus est*. This type of future-exponent remained in use until very late, though it is not reflected in Romance. Again, in the highly colloquial letter 471 there are two instances (in a quotation of direct speech) of the use of the present indicative with future reference: 24 f. *spec[t]emus illum dum uenit et uen[i]o tequm Alexandrie et* deduco *te usque ad naue*. So in the *Peregrinatio Aetheriae* this usage is confined to direct speech.[44] It also occurs in the Greek letters (476.19 ἀποτάσσομαι).

Missiturum (468.22) and *[u]iciturum* (468.37) show remodelling of the classical future participle (based, of course, on the past participle).

The augmented past participle suffixes *-ātus*, *-ītus* and *-ūtus*, all carrying the accent, became the most productive types in the transition to Romance.[45] Though some participles with *-tus* (*-sus*) attached to a consonantal stem survived, they were often replaced (e.g. *capitus = captus, sepelitus = sepultus, etc.). The *-ĭtus* type probably seen here tended to disappear, but in early Vulgar Latin at least it seems to have shown some productivity. *Vinciturum* = *uicturum* occurs in Petronius (45.10), *subscribituris* in the Tablettes Albertini (IV.3), *tulitus* in the fourth century translation of parts of Babrius (Cavenaile (1958), 40.7), and *probitus* = *probatus* in inscrip-

---

[44] Löfstedt (1911), 213.
[45] For many of the examples discussed in this section see Grandgent (1907), 183 ff.; Bourciez (1946), 226 f.; Väänänen (1965), 36.

tions (*CIL* v.896, 8278). Grandgent (1907), 184, also mentions a few other new formations. A majority of the future participles in the letters happen to have the termination *-iturus*, a fact which helps to explain the analogical remodelling (cf. 467.8 *exiturum*, 471.14 f. *exiturum*, 24 *abit[u]ri*, 33 *abiturum*; the only exception in the letters of Terentianus is *missurus* at 467.23, though in the letter of Tiberianus *uenturus* occurs twice (472.4, 11), *daturus* once (15) and *missurus* once (17)).

It was the stem of the infectum rather than the root which came to form the base of the past participle in Vulgar Latin. Different bases are rare (but note *tulitus* above; cf. *uixutus = *uictus*). Hence participles which originally dropped a nasal infix in the perfectum (e.g. *fractus*, *strictus*) were rebuilt on the infectum (*franctus, *strinctus). So *missus* was in some areas modified to *mittutus (>OSp. *metudo*, OIt. *mettuto*, etc.). Clearly a type of proportional analogy operates when one of the augmented suffixes is attached to the present stem. The analogy is founded on an analysis such as *am-at* → *am-atus* (hence, for example, *sepel-it* → *sepel-itus*). Petronius' *uinciturum* and *subscribituris* above are of this type.

But analogy is not always exactly proportional. Often an old form felt to be anomalous is not replaced (as was *sepultus*) but covered over. So the productive Vulgar Latin perfect suffix *-ui* was sometimes attached not to the present stem (replacement: see, for example, *cadui = *cecidi*, *capui* = *cepi*; see Grandgent (1907), 181, for examples), but to the existing perfect stem (covering over: e.g. *CIL* III.6010,137 *fecuit*; cf. *uēnui, *uīdui alongside *uĭdui, etc.; in children's English contrast *feets* alongside the proportional *foots*). Such is the modification which *missiturum* has undergone. The old participle *missus* lurks beneath the new. It is to be observed that *missiturum* is different in type from *tulitus*, in that it is not the stem of the perfectum which has provided the base.

Viciturum also seems to show covering over of the old participle. Alternatively the base may be a back-formation from *uixi*. The perfect marker *s* might have been removed to give a new present stem *uic-* (on the analogy, for example, of *dixi–dico*). Contrast the formation from *fixi, fictus* of a new present *figo* to replace old Latin *fiuo*.

A clear indication of the lack of currency of the future passive infinitive is furnished by 468.36 ff., where a present passive infinitive is in coordination with a future active: *spero me frugaliter [u]iciturum et in cohortem [tra]nsferri*.[46]

At 468.40 the editors emend *ualunt* to *ualebunt*. 468.38 ff. thus runs as follows: *hic a[ut]em sene aer[e] [ni]hil fiet neque epistulae commandaticiae nihil ual⟨eb⟩unt nesi si* . . . But Pighi (1964, 54) is undoubtedly right in noting that a future is not convincing here. It is better to retain *ualunt* and treat *fiet* as a present (= 'here nothing is achieved without money, and letters of recommendation are of no value'). *Fiet* is used twelve times as a present in the *Compositiones Lucenses*.[47] The monosyllable *fit* presumably lacked currency. *Fiet* was able to be reinterpreted partly because *-et* was a common present termination,[48] and partly because it was ceasing to be a distinctive future morph.

Valunt poses no problems. There is haphazard interchange of terminations between second and third conjugation verbs in vulgar texts (hence *-ent* for *-unt*).[49]

ii Present historic

The present historic is certain only with *uerba dicendi*: 467.9 *ait mihi*, 469.14 *dico illei et ego*, 470.24 *dicet*,[50] 471.10 *dico illi, da mi, di[c]o, a[e]s paucum; ibo, dico, ad amicos*, 27 *dico illi*, 31 *dico illi*, 33 *dicet*. It seems likely that a vivid present was in common use in the retailing of conversations (cf. *Anon. Vales*. 61). The pleonastic repetition of *dico* at 471.10 is of a type familiar in vulg. English (cf. Plaut. *Mil*. 61 ff.).

---

[46] Cf. Calderini (1951), 261. On the replacement of the future passive by the present passive infinitive, see Hofmann and Szantyr (1965), 358.

[47] See Svennung (1941), 128 f.

[48] Note that in the *Compositiones Lucenses -ent* often replaces *-unt*: Svennung (1941), 128.

[49] Grandgent (1907), 167.   [50] Perhaps a future.

It is also possible that *parit* at 471.20 is an historic present: *dende pos paucos dies parit, et non poterat mihi succurrere*. But since it is surrounded by verbs in past tenses, it was probably intended as a perfect. The reduplicated perfects were gradually eliminated from the verb system. In the Reichenau Glosses *tetigit* is glossed by *tangit*, and *ceciderunt* by *caderunt* (showing the attachment of perfect terminations to the present stem).[51] *Peperit* is one of the reduplicated perfects which is glossed in the same glossary.[52]

iii Perfect

The letters provide no worthwhile evidence concerning the remodelling of the perfect system. Aoristic perfects are common, but the synthetic perfective is found only once (467.13 *nullus [co]mputauit kasus su̱[ae] u̱[itae]*).[53] Alongside this the periphrastic perfective turns up once: 468.33 *te̱ ha̱[b]ere bo̱[na] re a̱ccept[am]*.[54]

iv Some morphological anomalies

merca (469.17).   Calderini (1951, 259) makes the strange assertion that *merca* stands for *mercatur*, 'fenomeno assai comune nel latino tardo' (but see Pighi (1964), 61). But it is a straightforward example of a deponent which has passed into the active (cf. It. *mercare*). Not much significance can be attached to this example, for it is the rare passive imperative which has been replaced. The rarer a form, the more likely it is to be remodelled. Deponents are still found in the letters (467.8, 17, 468.24, 470.25, 472.11).

posso (469.15).   It is unlikely that this form is due to loss of final /m/ and the merger of /u/ and /ō/. As we have seen, there is no sure example in the letters of ⟨o⟩ for /u/ in a final syllable

---

[51] Elcock (1960), 316.   [52] See Rohlfs (1969), 59.
[53] There are inevitably a few perfects which are difficult to classify (e.g. 467.4 *accepis[se]*).
[54] In the Greek letters cf. 476.17 ($\H{\epsilon}\chi\omega$ + participle). But the synthetic perfect is still common.

accompanied by the loss of ⟨-m⟩. It is rather a morphological regularisation. It is *potere* that Romance forms reflect.[55] But before the regularised forms of the Latin irregular verbs were stabilised in Vulgar Latin, there may have been a variety of remodelled forms in existence. Though *uelle* was ultimately replaced by **uolere*,[56] *uellere* was also in use for a while (e.g. *Vet. Lat.* Luke 6:1 (*b*, *d*), Fredegar, p. 147.4). *Posso* occurs in Gregory of Tours, Fredegar and another papyrus.[57]

collexi (471.12 f.). Perfects formed with long grade of the root were remade in Vulgar Latin by the attachment of the productive suffixes *-ui* or *-si* to either the old perfect stem or to the stem of the infectum (e.g. **uenui* = *ueni*, **capui* = *cepi*, **franxi* = *fregi*: see above, p. 50).[58] Our example confirms (cf. *CIL* III.12484, VI.406) that *lexi* = *legi* was in use in Vulgar Latin as an alternative to *legui* (see *CIL* VIII.20394 *legueris*).

v Present participle

The letters furnish some negative evidence concerning the present participle. The participial system of classical Latin rarely finds its way into the more mundane varieties of Latin at any period,[59] though in late vulgar texts the present participle shows a temporary tendency to move into the gap caused by the absence of a perfective active participle, and thereby to form a system with the perfect (passive) participle.[60] Terentianus hardly ever uses the present participle (on a past participial construction, the ablative absolute, see below, III.8). There are examples at 468.13 (*iacentem*) and 470.21 (*pergentes*), and possibly another at 471.33 (*mater ma no⟨n haben⟩s assem*). The Latin letters contrast sharply with the Greek, where participles are common. It would seem that it was the asymmetry of the Latin system (compared with the

---

[55] Meyer-Lübke (1935), 6682.   [56] Meyer-Lübke (1935), 9180.
[57] Cavenaile (1958), 192.16 (A.D. 167). Cf. Grandgent (1907), 168.
[58] See Grandgent (1907), 181; Bourciez (1946), 83 f. for examples.
[59] Hofmann and Szantyr (1965), 383 f.
[60] Hofmann and Szantyr (1965), 387.

greater symmetry of the Greek) which caused its lack of currency in popular speech.

The sense requires that *exiendo* at 471.31 (*attonitus exiendo dico illi*) be taken as equivalent to the dative of the present participle (*exeunti*). The oblique cases of the present participle of *ire* tended to be reshaped on the analogy of *iens* (*ient-*: note *CIL* v.7464 *praeterientes* = *praetereuntes*; cf. *TLL* v.2.626.52). It is *exienti* which underlies *exiendo* here. The ending may have been contaminated with that of the ablative of the gerund (*exeundo*),[61] presumably because the latter was overlapping in function at this time with the present participle. Cf. *babbandam*, Cavenaile (1958), 40.30: though the verb is unknown, it is intended as a present participle translating φέρουσαν.

              vi   me calcio *(468.26)*

Calcio is sometimes used in the passive with reflexive sense (e.g. Plin. *Nat.* 7.181 *dum calciantur*; cf. Plin. *Nat.* 8.215). But the encroachment of reflexive pronouns on the medio-passive was constant in Latin, and it is not surprising that in a vulgar text the reflexive expression should be used (*bis me im mensem calcio*).

4 CONJUNCTIONS

The temporal use of *quando* at 471.27 (*illa die qu[a]ndo tam magna lites factam est*) is a colloquialism avoided by Caesar, Varro and Sallust and used by Cicero only in his early works and in archaising passages.[62] In late vulgar texts it is common, and in Romance along with *quomodo* it ousts *cum* (cf. It. *quando*, Fr. *quand*) (note *Vit. Patr.* 5.5.27 *quando separatus sum a te* = 3.12 *cum separatus fuissem a te*).

Cum does not appear in the letters.[63] We have seen above

---

[61] On this usage, and its Romance importance, see, e.g., Elcock (1960), 111 f.
[62] Hofmann and Szantyr (1965), 607.
[63] Note that at 467.4 *quotiens* rather than the iterative use of *cum* occurs.

that one of its replacements is the better motivated *quo tempus*. Its absence would appear to anticipate the Romance situation.

Quoniam is used twice (467.15, 21), though in the *Cena Trimalchionis* it does not occur. In Livy the word is found mainly in speeches,[64] a fact which suggests that at this period it may have been domiciled in some spoken varieties of Latin, despite its absence from the *Cena*. Causal *quod* occurs at 468.7, but *quia* is not used.

At 471.25 *dum* ('until') is used after a *uerbum exspectandi* with an indicative verb (*spec[t]emus illum dum uenit*). This usage was almost certainly a colloquialism at this time. In such contexts Cicero employs a subjunctive verb, except occasionally in the early works and in the letters.[65] The evidence of our letters confirms that of Cicero. The same construction also occurs in comedy (Ter.*Eun*. 206 *exspectabo dum uenit*). Thus there was continuity in the spoken language between old Latin and the early Empire.

Modo si is used with the same function as the classical *si modo* at 468.21 (*modo si non iacu̯[i]sse*) (cf. 5395.8). Again the letters allow us to establish a continuity between the Vulgar Latin of the early Republic and of the late Empire. *Modo si* occurs in Plautus (*Capt*. 996 *modo si infectum fieri possiet!*) and then, apart from in poetry, not until late Latin.[66]

Nisi si (468.40 f. *nesi si qui sibi aiutaueret*) is a colloquialism.[67]

On *uide si*, see below, III.10.

At 471.15 the editors restore the conjunction *quamquam* (as well as inserting *dedit*): *item non mi d[e]dit aes quam⟨quam⟩ aureum matri mee in vestimenta ⟨dedit⟩*. Both changes are unnecessary. *Item ... quam* is to be taken as a correlative expression (= 'he did not give me money, as he

---

[64] See Hofmann and Szantyr (1965), 627.
[65] Hofmann and Szantyr (1965), 616.
[66] Hofmann and Szantyr (1965), 673.
[67] Hofmann and Szantyr (1965), 668.

gave my mother an *aureus* for clothing'), and *dedit* can be readily supplied from the first clause.

5 ADJECTIVES

i tam magnus *(471.27)*

Used for *tantus* (*qu[a]ndo tam magna lites factam est*). This usage survives in Sp. *tamaño* (cf. *CIL* vi.14672.12 *in tam mana clade*).⁶⁸ There are a few examples in Cicero, Petronius, Vitruvius and others, but it was clearly not domiciled in educated varieties of the language (see *TLL* vii.142.47 ff.).

The second element of the comparison (which might have been introduced by correlative *quam*) is not expressed. Deletion of such complements (whether they be correlative or consecutive) is characteristic of colloquial speech (cf. Eng. 'such a nice day', 'she is so nice'). In structures of this type *tam* + adjective is virtually the equivalent of an emphatic superlative. Cf. Pctron. 42.3 *homo bellus, tam bonus Chrysanthus animam ebulliit*. Genuine synthetic superlatives (adjectival or adverbial) in the letters are confined to epistolary formulae: 467.1 f. *patri karissimo plurimam salutem* (so 469.2, 472.2); 7 *optime scis* (so 472.3); 468.3 f. *que m[ihi ma]xime uota [su]nt*; 468.64 f. *bene ualere te opto multis annis felicissime im perpetuo*. See further below, iii.6.ii, on *perbene . . . recte* (468.47 f.).

ii praegnatam *(471.19)*

This form is due to contamination of *praegnans* with *natus*.

6 ADVERBS

i crebrum *(472.23)*

If the reading is right, *c̣[r]eḅruṃ* (*c̣[r]eḅruṃ salutat te Claud[i]us*) raises the problem of the adverbial use of neuter accusatives of adjectives and pronouns. In Latin there are not

---

⁶⁸ See Löfstedt (1933–42), ii, 339.

a great many usages of this type, and it is often difficult to decide whether those which do occur are Grecisms or genuine Latin adverbials.[69] It is not the plural use which is problematical: adverbials such as *multa*, *magna*, *grandia*, etc., are poetical and Grecising.

Certain neuter singulars of quantity seem to have been well established in Latin of all types from Plautus onwards (*multum*, *nimium*, *magnum*, *maximum*; note Cic. *Tusc.* 2.5 *exclamare maius*). Similarly in Vulgar Latin there were various equivalent intensives consisting not of quantitative adjectives but of adjectives of emotion and the like (e.g. Plaut. *Mil.* 24 *insanum*, Petron. 68.7 *desperatum*).[70]

Adverbial neuters with a temporal or iterative sense (as *crebrum*) are more difficult to interpret. *Hibernum* occurs in Plautus (*Rud.* 69), but it is in a prologue where the possibility of Greek influence must be admitted.[71] Most parallels are found mainly or exclusively in poetry. Hofmann and Szantyr (1965, 40) are inclined to accept *aeternum* as a genuine Latinism, but it occurs in prose only in Tacitus, who of course is well known for his poeticising tendencies. Plautus (*Aul.* 147) uses *sempiternum*, but again there is the possibility of Greek influence (cf. συνεχὲς αἰεί, ἐμμενὲς αἰεί).

In the absence of a reasonable number of temporal neuters in non-artificial prose where the influence both of Greek and of poetry is unlikely, it must be concluded that *crebrum* here is a Grecism (cf. συχνόν) rather than a native Latin usage with any currency in Vulgar Latin. Another example is quoted at *TLL* IV.1121.64 ff., but it is in the poetry of Paulinus of Nola and was undoubtedly a Grecising poeticism. There are also plural examples in Lucretius (2.359), Virgil (*Georg.* 3.500) and Apuleius (*Met.* 2.17). These too are obviously poetical.

---

[69] Most of the examples dealt with here are mentioned by Hofmann and Szantyr (1965), 40; Löfstedt (1933–42), II, 418 ff.

[70] These adjectives are used to modify adjectives and adverbs (i.e. as superlative-substitutes) rather than verbs. See Hofmann and Szantyr (1965), 163.

[71] Hofmann and Szantyr (1965), 40.

ii perb[e]ne ... recte *(468.47 f.)*

I interpret *perbene* as a modifier of *recte* (*perb[e]ne omnia recte esse*) and the expression as a substitute for a synthetic superlative. Combinations comprising *bene* + adjective or adverb are common in colloquial texts. *Bene magnus, bene firmus* and *bene multi* all occur in the *B. Hisp.*[72] Cf., e.g., Plaut. *Capt.* 966 *bene morigerus fuit*; Cic. *Att.* 4.9.2. *bene mane*. Cf. Fr. *bien*, It. *bene*.

The formation *per* + adjective or adverb was of course very productive in the spoken registers. *Perbene* is found once in Cicero's letters (*Fam.* 13.16.1) and at *Brut.* 108, but not in the speeches. So *perbelle* is found in the letters.

iii celerius

Tiberianus three times uses *celerius* instead of a positive: 472.4 *celerius at [t]e uenturum*; 9 f. *occasione inuenta spero me celerius aput te uenturum*; 13 *[ut i]hi te possi[m inu]enire c[el]er̯[iu]s*. This usage is especially characteristic of Vulgar Latin, though it is not restricted to vulgar texts.[73] In both Greek and Latin the comparative can have an oppositional value. οἱ πρεσβύτεροι may mean not 'older men' in reference to other old men, but 'old men' in contrast to 'young men' (οἱ νεώτεροι).[74] *Celerius* is contrastive with (e.g.) *lentius*. Thus orders of the form *abi hinc intro ocius* (Plaut. *Merc.* 930) mean 'don't be slow'. The suffix **-ero* (or **t-ero*), which was used in Greek to form the comparative, appears in Latin in certain oppositions similar to those above: *magister–minister, dexter–sinister, noster–uester, superus–inferus*.[75]

An identical usage occurs in one of the Greek letters: 479.12 ff. πᾶν δὲ ποι⟨η⟩σάτω ἀναδοῦναι αὐτὴν ταχύτερον τῷ στρατηγῷ.

---

[72] Hofmann (1951), 74.
[73] Hofmann and Szantyr (1965), 168 f.
[74] See Mayser (1906–34), II, 1, 47 f.
[75] See Monteil (1974), 210 f.

7 PARTICLES

Connective particles are not as common in ordinary speech as in the literary varieties of a language. Yet in most late vulgar texts they are used incessantly, no doubt because of the literary aspirations of most authors of such works. In the letters there are few particles. In this respect too the letters probably take us closer to popular speech than the speeches of the freedmen in the *Cena Trimalchionis*, who are constantly given particles by Petronius.

Even the adversatives *at* and *sed* are absent entirely, and *enim* occurs only four times (467.18, 469.11, 12, 18). It is only *autem* which is used with any frequency (ten times: 467.4, 6, 8, 22, 468.12, 25, 34, 38, 471.18 f.), with a variety of functions. It is probably adversative at 467.6 *t]u autem dedisti illis aspros*, 468.25 *caligae autem nucl[e]atae nugae sunt* and 471.18 f. *matrem meam aute praegnatam imueni*, but it is usually either connective or explanatory (= *enim*).[76] In all of these functions the word is found in the classical period, though it is sometimes erroneously stated that the classical function was the adversative and that the others were a feature of later Latin.[77]

8 ABSOLUTE CONSTRUCTIONS

At 468.13 (*et me iacentem in liburna sublata mi s[unt]*; cf. 5395.4) *me iacentem* is absolute in the sense that it has no grammatical connection with the rest of the sentence. But it would be a mistake to call it an accusative absolute. This expression is best reserved for the intentional use of an accusatival construction with a function the same as that of the classical ablative absolute. In late Latin absolute uses of accusatival constructions are frequent enough,[78] and they

---

[76] Connective: 467.4, 8, 22, 468.12; explanatory 468.34, 38.
[77] For the connective and explanatory uses, see *TLL* II.1588.34 ff.
[78] See Ernout and Thomas (1953), 24; Hofmann and Szantyr (1965), 143; Norberg (1943), 87 ff.

may have been deliberate. But there is no evidence for them in the early period. It is better to explain this example as a case of anacolouthon. Terentianus had a vague conception of himself as the patient of a verbal action (e.g. *me iacentem aliquis priuauit culcita et pulbino*), but he lapsed into the passive because the author of the action was unknown. Hence the accusative expression was left unattached. Contamination of active and passive structures is very common in texts of vulgar flavour. Often, for example, the substantival component of an ablative absolute (which is usually a passive structure) is placed in the accusative instead of the ablative because the underlying active structure is contaminated with the required passive structure (e.g. *Anon. Vales.* 63 *accepta uxorem*: contamination of *accepta uxore* and *ille accepit uxorem*).

Anacolouthon and contamination are only to be expected in Latin of this type. Cf. 472.17 ff. [a]ṭ ṭe ṃiṣṣuro [mí]ḥi et epi[st]u[la]s ḍuas quas [c]ụpias acuṃ[in]ẹ [et fo]rṭuna a[pu]ḍ [i]llụm re[pe]rṭạ[s t]ibi remisi s[i]g[n]aṭas. Tiberianus sets out to refer to himself in an oblique case (*missuro mihi*), but then changes the cast of the sentence so that he himself is the subject (*remisi*). Similarly 471.29 (*non magis qurauit me pro xylesphongium*) exhibits contamination of *non magis curauit me quam xylesphongium* and *habuit me pro xylesphongio* (so the editors). See further below, III.9 on 468.27 ff. and 467.17.

It is possible that *me iacentem* was conceived as an ablative absolute, and that ⟨-m⟩ was haphazardly added as at 471.27 (so the editors; cf. Pighi (1964),48). If so, the construction is one of those illogical examples, so common in vulgar texts,[79] which the writer could have avoided by placing the participle in another case in agreement with an existing nominal component of the sentence (*mihi iacenti sublata sunt*). However, the only sure example of an ablative absolute in the letters is at 472.9 f. (*occasione inuenta*) in the letter of Tiberianus, whose Latin, as we have seen, is more learned than that of Terentianus. Moreover *occasione inuenta* was a common

---

[79] Hofmann and Szantyr (1965), 139 f.

cliché (cf. *Anon. Vales.* 85). The ablative absolute was a literary construction. It is better therefore to explain the oddity as due to anacolouthon.

However *me iacentem* is regarded, the letters furnish new evidence for the rarity of the ablative absolute in Vulgar Latin.[80]

9 ACCUSATIVE AND DATIVE WITH THE INFINITIVE

A notable absence from the letters is the use of object clauses (introduced by *quod* or *quia*) for the acc. + infin. The latter is used with considerable freedom, but there is no example of an object clause. Either the acc. + infin. still enjoyed some vitality in Vulgar Latin (at least in the circles in which Terentianus moved), perhaps with minimal overlap from object clauses (which would explain the occasional examples in Petronius (note 46.4, 71.9) and other early writers), or Terentianus employed the acc. + infin. as a literary affectation. But we have seen little trace of learned affectation or hyperurbanism in the letters. Moreover Terentianus was a bilingual who made use of ὅτι clauses in his Greek letters. At 476.17 and 477.28, for instance, ὅτι constructions depend on οἶδα, whereas in the Latin letters the acc. + infin. is constantly employed with *scio* (467.4, 8, 26, 468.4, 43, 47). Had *quod* or *quia* clauses had any currency in Latin, we should have expected the existence of the Greek ὅτι construction to have provided an additional impulse for a bilingual to admit object clauses in Latin. The isolated examples of object clauses in early vulgar texts should not therefore be treated as the tip of an iceberg. Object clauses for the acc. + infin. must have become established fairly late in Vulgar Latin.

Some examples of the acc. + infin. were clearly of a type formulaic in epistolography. But there remain sufficient instances to show that the construction was at home in the

---

[80] Cf. Väänänen (1967), 178 f.

spoken registers of the author. *Opto te fortem* (467.2) was obviously formulaic: it corresponds to a similar formula in the Greek letters (e.g. 476.2 εὔχομαί σε ὑγιαίνειν). Cf. *opto te bene ualere* (468.3, 64). Another repeated cliché is *scias omnia recte esse* (467.26, 468.47 f.).

There is a peculiar instance of an acc. + infin. at 468.27 ff. which does not have a governing verb: *ea q[u]am mi misisti optionem illan mi ab[s]tulisse*. Calderini (1951, 261) tentatively suggests that this may be a case of the accusative of exclamation. But in the examples quoted of this construction the subject accusative regularly precedes the verb and comes at the head of the construction.[81] It is unlikely that here we have an anomalous example in which the initial position is occupied by the object of the verb. It is simpler to suppose that Terentianus departed from his usual practice and set out in this sentence to postpone the governing verb (*scias*, which, as we have seen, occurs repeatedly in the letters with a dependent acc. + infin., would give perfect sense), but because of the abnormality of the order neglected to add it. The sentence thus contains an error of omission rather than a case of anacolouthon. That the order V + acc. + infin. was the one with which Terentianus was most familiar can be seen from a glance at the rest of the letters (see below, IV.5).

Though object clauses have made no inroads on the acc. + infin., there is one favoured alternative to it which distinguishes the Latin from that of classical prose. With only three exceptions (467.9, 469.12, 471.32), when the verb is one of saying Terentianus prefers quoted direct speech: e.g. 471.10 *dico illi, da mi, di[c]o, a̧[e]s paucum*; *ibo, dico, ad amicos*; 24 *mater mea*: *spec[t]emus illum dum uenit* (note that there is no need to supply, with the editors, *dicit* after *mea*; ellipse of a verb of saying is very common:[82] e.g. *CIL* VIII.292 *D.m.s. Catilius se uibum fecissse*; cf. Petron. 47.11). Cf. 467.9, 469.14, 470.24, 471.16, 27, 31, 33. In two of the three exceptional cases the verb is *nego*. Only 469.12 remains, and

---

[81] Hofmann and Szantyr (1965), 48; Ernout and Thomas (1953), 23 f.
[82] Löfstedt (1933–42), II, 244 ff.

there *diceba[t]* follows the acc. + infin.: the construction is literary, as the abnormal order shows.

At 467.17 (*ne tib̩[i] pareaṃ a spe aṃar̩[a] par̩pa[tum] u̩agari quasi fugitiuom*) an acc. + infin. is used instead of a plain infinitive. This is a common type of vulgarism which arises from the contamination of the personal construction with the impersonal.[83]

Another passage worthy of note is at 468.43 ff.: *ed [sci]as Carpum hic errasse, ed in̩u̩[e]ntus est Dios in legione, et a[cce]pisse me pr̩o il̩lo* (*denarios*) *VI*. The second clause should presumably be part of the indirect construction,[84] but instead the writer has lapsed into the indicative. A tolerably close parallel to the process involved here is provided by the treatment of the second of two co-ordinated object clauses dependent on *uerba dicendi* in the *Vitae Patrum*. Often the first clause has a subjunctive verb because of the feeling that the subjunctive was the mood appropriate to indirect statement, but the second, at a greater remove from the governing verb and with its dependence less strongly felt, has an indicative verb, e.g. 5.15.29 *dicebant de abbate Moyse quia factus esset clericus, et posuerunt ei superhumerale*. There is a close parallel to our example in the Greek letters: 477.32 ff. [γ]εινώσκειν σε θέλω . . . ἐνηνεγμένον μοι . . . τὸ καλάθιον, καὶ τὸ τέ[λο]ς νοῖν πά[ρεσ]τ̩ιν ἐ̩[μο]ί̩.

At 471.21 f. (*et factum est illi uenire Alexandrie*) an infinitive standing as complement of a verb has displaced the classical complement *ut* + subj. Such displacement was a feature of the historical development of Latin. *Factum est* + infin. is quoted only a few times by *TLL* VI.1.101.79 ff., first from the *Itala* and then Victor Vitensis.

The dependent construction is dat. + infin. instead of the expected acc. + infin. The construction dat. + infin. arises from a straightforward type of contamination. The expression

---

[83] See Hofmann and Szantyr (1965), 357, for some comparable examples, all late, of *uideor* with an accusative and infinitive.

[84] Pighi (1964), 55, however, believes that the indirect statement was temporarily suspended.

difficile est, for example, could be complemented either by a dative (e.g. *natatio illi est difficilis*) or by an acc. + infin. (e.g. *difficile est illum natare*). By conflation the pattern *difficile est illi natare* emerges in late Latin (*TLL* v.1.1084.22 ff.).[85] The dat. + infin. is more familiar in Greek, where there may be overlapping between an acc. + infin. and a dat. + infin. συνέβη, for instance, takes both constructions: e.g. Hdt. 6.103 συνέβη αὐτῷ 'Ολυμπιάδα ἀνελέσθαι; cf. 7.166 συνέβη Γέλωνα νικᾶν. The construction used by Terentianus could represent a genuine Latin development, or it may have been due to Greek influence.

10 INDIRECT QUESTIONS

Just as the governing verb in indirect statement usually precedes the acc. + infin., so in indirect questions (and commands) the governing verb precedes the dependent clause (see below, IV.5).

There are two examples of indirect questions[86] in which the verb is indicative rather than subjunctive, in the manner typical of Vulgar Latin:[87] 469.6 f. *uide si potes imbenire*; 472.12 *rescribere ubi constas*. I exclude 467.7 (*optime scis et tu quantum col[legis suis m]entitus*), because the text is uncertain. The first example, with its conjunction *si* instead of *num*, is a type of expression found in old Latin and no doubt current in Vulgar Latin: cf. Ter. *Eun.* 838 *uide, amabo, si non, quom aspicias, os inpudens uidetur*. For *uideo* introducing other types of indirect question with indicative verbs, cf. Plaut. *Most.* 1172 *uiden ut adstat furcifer*; Cic. *Att.* 1.1.4 *uides . . . in quo cursu sumus. Si*, which turns up sporadically at all periods (though perhaps predominating in colloquial and late texts) at the head of indirect questions, survives with this function in Romance.[88]

[85] Cf. Hofmann and Szantyr (1965), 363.
[86] One of which was missed by Calderini (1951), 261.
[87] Hofmann and Szantyr (1965), 537 f.
[88] Hofmann and Szantyr (1965), 543 f. On the expression *uide si*, see Löfstedt (1911), 327 f.

11 NEGATION

At 468.39 f. (*neque epistulae commandaticiae nihil ualunt*) there is an example of pleonastic negation of a type common in Vulgar Latin.[89] For *nec* followed by a negative, cf. Petron. 58.5 *nec deorsum non cresco*, and for *nihil* following another negative, cf. Petron. 42.7 *neminem nihil boni facere oportet*.

[89] On the whole question, see Löfstedt (1933–42), II, 209 ff.

IV WORD ORDER

The word order of the letters raises acutely the question of the possible influence of Greek on Terentianus' Latin (or vice versa). The Latin letters already display a number of the patterns characteristic of late Latin and Romance. But much the same patterns are also found in the Greek letters, and we must therefore admit the possibility of Greek influence. A bilingual may well impose the patterns of one language on another.[1] However, the Latin letters are by no means empty of distinctive Latin traits: hence even if there is Greek influence on them, they cannot be regarded as completely abnormal. They were certainly the work of a man fluent in Latin.

Nevertheless there is one apparent Grecising feature to be seen in the Latin letters, against which can be set no Latinising feature in the Greek letters. The picture is complex. Terentianus was familiar with Latin patterns, and it is therefore likely that in general the word order which he used in the Latin letters was representative of genuine spoken Latin. The similarity between his Greek and Latin word order may to a large extent be due to parallel development of the two languages (indeed, typological study establishes that Latin and Greek did develop along the same lines in word order: see below). On the other hand, if the presence of a Greek characteristic in the Latin letters is accepted it becomes likely that Greek was Terentianus' usual language. But the evidence is far from clear-cut (see below on object and pronoun position).

The evidence concerning word order furnished by the let-

[1] See Weinreich (1953), 37 f.

ters is of considerable importance both from a typological point of view and for the light which it throws on the relationship between popular speech and the literary registers at this period. For the first time we are given a clear indication of the gulf which existed between popular patterns and those of literature. The Pompeian inscriptions are so short that it is pointless to examine their word order. And in the speeches of the freedmen in the *Cena Trimalchionis* Petronius did not depart from the patterns of the learned narrative.

It has recently been suggested that in word order languages can be divided into two groups.[2] On the one hand are those in which the object precedes the verb, and on the other those with the order VO. If the object (which may be said to limit or modify the verb) precedes the verb, other limiting or modifying elements also tend to precede the element modified. The genitive precedes its noun, relative clauses precede the antecedent, adjectives precede their noun, and so on. On the other hand in a VO language modifiers come after the element modified.

Latin, like other Western IE languages,[3] changed from an OV to a VO type. Late vulgar texts, like the Romance languages, are VO in character, but earlier (in the Republican and early Imperial periods) literary texts show marked OV characteristics. The verb, for instance, in Caesar, Cicero and many others habitually follows the object.[4] Similarly the high incidence of old genitival formulae with the order genitive + noun (e.g. *senatus consultum*, *senatus auctoritas*, *senatus sententia*, *plebi scitum*, gen. + *causa* and *gratia*, *pro deum atque hominum fidem*, *Luci filius*, *iuris consultus*, *operae pretium est*, etc.) points to the original OV state of the language.

The letters of Terentianus are the first text extant to exhibit extensive VO features, in anticipation of Romance. Yet at

---

[2] See Lehmann (1972), (1974). Lehmann has extended the work of Greenberg (1966). I have dealt in detail with the Latin evidence elsewhere (Adams (forthcoming, *a*)), and can only allude here to the change which Latin underwent.

[3] See Lehmann (1972), 976 f.   [4] Hofmann and Szantyr (1965), 403.

much the same time Tacitus, for example, and Suetonius were preserving the OV patterns of an earlier period. The spoken language of the uneducated had evidently already changed in type, whereas in literature OV patterns were retained as prestigious.

Here I consider (among other things) the position of the object, genitive, adjective, dependent infinitive, embedded object sentences, prepositional adjuncts (adverbials) and relative clauses, all of which would be expected to follow their associated element in a VO language.

1 OBJECT POSITION

The order VO outnumbers OV by 40:14 in the Latin letters, and by 33:16 in the Greek. In the Latin VO is preferred in the proportion of roughly 2:1 both when the verb is finite (23:9) and when it is an infinitive (8:4). By contrast it is preferred by 9:1 when the verb is imperative. There had always been a marked tendency for imperatives to precede their object.

In the Greek letters VO predominates by 14:5 when the verb is finite and 9:3 when it is imperative, but when it is an infinitive anteposition is as common as postposition (5:5). Thus the predominance in the Latin of VO when the verb is an infinitive could be a genuine Latin characteristic.

Certain Greek epistolary formulae which were taken over in the Latin letters have the order VO. Clearly in these cases Greek influence must be allowed, though since VO was probably the norm in Vulgar Latin also, the structure of the formulae would scarcely have seemed unusual to a Latin speaker. Note the following correspondences:

467.5   me . . . accepis[se . . . ana]boladum
476.6   κεκομίσ[θ]αι με . . . καλάθιον
467.27 [m]isi tibi amphoras II oliuarum
481.19 ἔπεμ[ψ]ά σοι ὀριγάνιν (cf. 35)
468.60 saluta Serenum
476.24 ἄσπασ[αι] Δίδυμον

There is one peculiarity in the Latin letters. In subordinate clauses the incidence of OV does not increase. In the Greek letters postposition of the object is preferred by 4:2, and in the Latin by 9:1. Yet in Latin of all periods, including that of late vulgar texts, the verb showed a considerably greater tendency to gravitate to the final position in subordinate clauses than it did in main clauses.[5] In the *Anonymus Valesianus*, for example, VO predominates by 37:26 in main clauses, yet in subordinate clauses OV is preferred by 21:6. The effects of this tendency were still felt to a limited extent in early Romance.[6] We shall see below traces of it in the Latin letters, but it is not as marked as would be expected. If the predominance of VO in subordinate clauses is not a statistical freak, it could be a Greek characteristic.[7] Indeed a case of VO at 467.30 f. can be compared with a very similar instance in a Greek letter: *or[o te] ... u]t ... mittas tr[e]s toc[adas*; cf. 477.27 ἐρω[τ]ῶ σε ἂν δύνῃ ... πέμψαι ὑπόδημα.

2 THE POSITION OF OBJECT PRONOUNS

There is no sign of Greek influence on pronoun position in the Latin letters. But a Latin characteristic is evident.

In both the Greek and Latin object (direct and indirect) pronouns have assumed an almost obligatory position next to the verb, whereas in literary Latin a lingering trace of the operation of Wackernagel's law often causes pronouns to be placed in the second position in their clause.[8] In the Latin letters juxtaposition predominates by 73:8, and in the Greek by 53:3. In the Latin most cases of pronouns which are separated from the verb are second word in the clause (468.7, 15, 26, 28, 469.15, 472.13).

In main clauses in both Greek and Latin postposition pre-

[5] Linde (1923), 154 ff.; Ramsden (1963), 43 f., 114.
[6] Ramsden (1963), 79, 88, 92 f., 98.
[7] The order OV does not appear to have been especially common in subordinate clauses in Greek: see the statistics given by Dover (1968), 29 f.
[8] See Ramsden (1963), 30, Adams (1976), 130 f., on the rarity of the separation of verb and object pronoun in vulgar texts.

dominates when the verb is finite (in Greek by 27:6 and in Latin by 36:8).[9] But in subordinate clauses in Latin it is anteposition which is preferred (14:6). This can only be put down to the Latin tendency for the verb in subordinate clauses to move towards the end of the clause. By contrast in the Greek letters postposition is the rule in subordinate (5:0) as well as main clauses.

It is distinctly possible that the order VO of main clauses had already been generalised in Vulgar Latin to subordinate clauses when O was nominal, but that the original subordinate clause pattern OV was retained when O was pronominal. Pronouns are notoriously resistant to the influence of order changes which a language might undergo. Indeed, in Romance weak object pronouns (unlike nominal objects) are still placed before the verb, though they may first have become postverbal before shifting back to the preverbal position.[10]

If generalisation of the order V + noun object had taken place in subordinate clauses, we could reject the possibility that in such clauses Terentianus was influenced by a Greek pattern. However, it remains puzzling that in much later vulgar texts such as the *Anonymus Valesianus* the order noun object + V is still preferred in subordinate clauses. On balance it seems likely that there is Greek interference in Terentianus.

In both the Greek and Latin letters there is a tendency for the object pronoun to precede the verb when it is an infinitive. Anteposition predominates by 6:3 in Latin and in Greek is as common as postposition (7:8).

3 THE GENITIVE

In both the Latin and Greek letters the habitual position of

---

[9] I include in these figures only examples of pronouns which are juxtaposed with the verb.

[10] I have elsewhere dealt in detail with pronoun position in late Latin (Adams (1976), 130 ff., *id*. (forthcoming, *b*), vii). Cf. Ramsden (1963), 112 ff.

the genitive is after the determinant. In the Latin postposition predominates by 7:3, and in the Greek by 39:10. The example of anteposition at 467.26 is in a formula (*deorum beneficio*) which usually shows this order (e.g. Cic. *Phil*. 3.33, 4.7, 5.23, 12.9, Liv. 28.35.8; cf. *TLL* II.1884. 74 ff.). That at 469.5 is also in a phrase with a formal ring (*Germani libertam*). In the Greek letters most of the anteposed genitives (seven) are personal pronouns.

The anteposition of *deorum* is clearly a genuine Latinism, and the anteposition of pronouns may be genuinely Greek. Parallel development of Greek and Latin had probably taken place.

4 ADJECTIVES

In (e.g.) French most adjectives follow their noun, though certain subjective, affective or emphatic adjectives precede. AN is the marked order, NA the unmarked. In the Latin letters NA outnumbers AN by 67:24. It is chiefly emphatic adjectives of size or quantity which occupy the marked position before the noun: e.g. *plurimus* (468.2, 469.2, 472.2), *multi* (467.36, 468.65), *magnus*, *maximus* (468.4, 471.27), *paucus* (471.13, 20), *minor* (469.7, 17), *omnes* (467.35, 468.61), *nullus* (471.3).

But in the Greek letters AN occurs eleven times, NA only eight.

5 THE INFINITIVE AND EMBEDDED OBJECT SENTENCES

In learned Latin dependent infinitives vary in position because of the needs of the rhythm of the clausula, though anteposition undoubtedly predominates. But in the Latin letters there are thirteen examples of infinitives (as primary complement) placed after the verb, but none of the order infin. + V: 467.29 p[ote]s et has cognoscere; 469.3 f. potes fieri; 6 f. potes imbenire; 14 nolim [pe]tere; 470.4 cup]it rog-

are; 471.19 *nil poterat facere*; 20 *non poterat mihi succurrere*; 23 *nihil poteramus facere*; 26 *paratus erat exire*; 28 *potes aiutare*; 31 *possim uenire*; 472.11 f. *digner[i]s . . . rescribere*; 13 *possi[m inu]enire*.

Similarly embedded sentences containing an infinitive (the acc. + infin. construction) regularly follow the main verb. There are twenty-one examples of the order V + (acc. + infin.), but only four of the alternative order. Two of these latter exceptions are in an epistolary formula: *bene ualere te opto* (467.35, 468.64). Another (468.12) is in one of the very few contexts in which Terentianus uses an acc. + infin. (as distinct from quoted direct speech) with a verb of saying (see above, III.9). There remains an example at 471.14 f., where an archaic verb (*siluit*, if the reconstruction of the text is correct) is placed in final position in the sentence.

Two other types of embedded sentences (indirect commands and indirect questions) also always follow the verb of the matrix sentence (eleven times).

6 PREPOSITIONAL ADJUNCTS

In classical Latin adverbials tended to precede the verb, as a result of the frequency with which the verb occupied final position. In Romance, however, they usually follow the verb.[11] In the letters the Romance situation has started to emerge. In the Greek letters prepositional expressions (which may be classified as adverbial, and will serve our purposes here) follow the verb fifty-nine times and precede it eighteen; and in the Latin postposition is preferred by 47:16.

7 RELATIVE CLAUSES

Every relative clause (of which there are nine) in the Latin letters follows its antecedent. Postposition is standard in VO

---

[11] See Ramsden (1963), 114, on the positioning of miscellaneous elements in the sentence. Cf. Adams (1976), 139, for some late Latin evidence.

languages. The earlier OV stage of Latin is most clearly exemplified in the Twelve Tables, where almost all relative clauses precede their antecedent.

8 VERB POSITION

In this section I deal with the incidence of final position compared with that of non-final position of the verb. No distinction is drawn between initial and medial position.

In the Greek letters the predominance of non-final position is roughly 5:1 (omitting from consideration examples of the copula). The figures are 64:12.

Final position of the verb had never been the rule in Greek, though it had in Latin. Hence it is not surprising to find that in the Latin letters final position is somewhat more numerous than in the Greek. Nevertheless it has been dislodged as the statistical norm. Overall non-final position is preferred by 94:36 (i.e. by less than 3:1).[12] These figures should be adjusted to 80:29 if the copula is to be omitted.[13]

In the Greek letters the incidence of final position is not altered in subordinate clauses. In main clauses final position is outnumbered by 42:8, and in subordinate clauses by 22:4.

On the other hand there is a slight difference between verb position in subordinate as distinct from main clauses in the Latin letters.[14] Non-final position is preferred by only 27:16 in subordinate clauses,[15] but by 55:20 in main clauses. But the increase in final position in subordinate clauses is less marked

[12] I include twelve instances of what appears to be non-final position in letter 470. But this letter is so fragmentary that there is often doubt about the exact position of the verb.
[13] A verb of saying or the like which is placed before the dependent construction but at the end of its clause is regarded as being in final position, though it does not end the sentence.
[14] I omit here the twelve examples of verbs in 470, where it is impossible to determine the nature of the clause, as well as examples of the copula.
[15] I omit the examples of final position at 467.23 (*et si quid missurus es*) and 467.24 (*ne quit mute*[*t*]*ur*), for *quid* almost obligatorily follows *si* or *ne*. The editors place *dedit* in final position at 471.16, but it could equally well have been placed elsewhere, and indeed is unnecessary in the context.

than might have been expected, especially if certain special cases are omitted.[16] It may well be that a genuine Latin feature is in evidence; but interference from Greek may have lessened its frequency.

Indeed, some of the relative clauses in the Latin letters have much the same structure as those in the Greek. The pattern relative + V + O, seen in the Greek at 476.7 (ἐν ᾧ εὗρον ἄρτους), turns up in the Latin at 468.9 f. (*in quo habes amicla*) and 16 (*in qua ha*[*bes*] *sunthe*[*seis*]).

On the other hand the pattern relative + object pronoun + V which occurs in the Latin letters may have been typical of Latin: 468.5 *quas mi misisti*; 7 f. *q*[*u*]*am mi misisti*; 469.8 f. *quas illei* [*a*]*ttuli*. With these examples contrast 480.13 ὃ δέδωκάς μοι. It would seem that in relative clauses there is a mixture of Latin and Greek patterns in the Latin letters, though the evidence is not such as to permit certainty.

In the following places a formula in Greek displaying non-final position of the verb is used with the same order in Latin:

468.46 sal[u]tat te mater mea (cf. 467.32, 469.3)
477.39 f. ἀσ]πάζεταί σε ... Ἰσίδω[ρος]

467.17 f. oro et rogo te ... (cf. 30, 468.20, 23, 470.21)
477.27 ἐρω[τ]ῶ σε

467.27 [m]isi tibi amphoras II oliuarum (cf. 468.8)
481.19 ἔπεμ[ψ]ά σοι ὀριγάνιν (cf. 481.35)

9 SUBJECT, VERB AND OBJECT

In the Latin letters the order SVO predominates when both O and S are expressed. It occurs ten times (six times in infinitival clauses), compared with four examples of VOS (all in the formula *salutat te* + S which is referred to above), one of OVS (471.20 f.), one of OSV (468.15: a special case, for *hunc* behaves as a relative), one of VSO (468.45), and three of SOV (two of which are in infinitival clauses).

---

[16] In a number of cases the verb occurs in final position in clauses in which there is only one other word, sometimes the subject (468.35 f.) – which

There are only eight places in the Greek letters where both S and O are expressed. SVO nowhere occurs. There are four examples of the formula ἀσπάζεταί σε + S, one of VSO, two of SOV and one of OSV (where O is emphatic: 476.19).

Thus the Latin letters show abundant characteristics typical of a VO language. Of particular note is the presence of the pattern SVO, which was later to become a syntactic order when S and O ceased to be flectionally distinct. How long before the time of Terentianus the unmarked patterns of ordinary speech diverged from those of educated writings it would be pointless to speculate here. But we can be grateful that the gulf can be established with certainty for as early as the start of the second century. In its conservative literary forms the language retained OV features for centuries after Terentianus.

Even if Greek interference is admitted, Terentianus was undoubtedly a fluent Latin speaker, a genuine bilingual rather than one who had learnt Latin late. The features of order in the Latin letters which reflect Latin usage are the archaic position of the genitive in the formula *deorum beneficio*, the slight increase in the incidence of final position of the verb in subordinate clauses, the order SVO, which is not found in the Greek letters, the greater frequency of NA in the Latin than in the Greek letters, and above all the different position of pronoun objects in subordinate as compared with main clauses.

almost inevitably precedes the verb – and sometimes a pronoun (468.23 f., 35, 41).

V VOCABULARY

1 ASPROS

According to the editors, *aspros* (467.6 *t*]*u autem dedisti illis aspros*; 9 *is*] *aute*[*m*] *negauit se habere aspros*) refers to garments of rough quality. This is possible, but another interpretation is also plausible, especially in view of Terentianus' complaints in another letter (471). *Asper* is habitually applied to new coin which has not been worn down, and by ellipse of a noun such as *nummus* there emerged a substantivised adjective = 'cash'. Indeed, ἄσπρα, a loan word from Latin, is found with this sense in NGr. It occurs as an adjective with syncopated form in the expression δηνάρια ἄσπρα at *IGR* ιν.494, as Cameron (1931, 238) notes. Cf. also *asprio* (*TLL* ιι.846.36 ff.) and *aspratura* (*TLL* ιι. 846.3 ff.). Note Pers. 3.69 f. *quid asper utile nummus habet*; Suet. *Ner.* 44.2 *nummum asperum*; *CGL* ιι.269.57 δηνάριον τραχὺ ἢ ἔκλευκον: *asprum*. There is a substantival use of the word at Sen. *Epist.* 19.10 *nec uoles quod debeo* ⟨*nisi*⟩ *in aspero et probo accipere*.

Similarly in 471 Terentianus complains that someone has refused to give him money: 10 ff. *da mi, di*[*c*]*o, a*[*e*]*s paucum; . . . nullum assem mi dedit*; 15 *item non mi d*[*e*]*dit aes*.

For the syncopated form, which is that of Romance reflexes (e.g. It. *aspro*, Rum. *aspru*),[1] see Prisc. *GL* ιι.225.14 *nam 'aspri' per syncopam dicitur* (cf. Scrib. Larg. 180, *Mul. Chir.* 58; *TLL* ιι.807.5).

---

[1] Meyer-Lübke (1935), 708.

2 BYRRVM (467.20)

A *birrus* was a hooded cloak in use under the Empire. The word is certainly a foreign borrowing, and probably Celtic (cf. Ir. *berr*).[2] At. Schol. Iuv. 8.145 it is given the epithet *Gallicus*. Moreover a number of loan words in Latin denoting garments were Celtic in origin (cf. *bracae, sagum*). *Birrus* survives in Romance (OProv. *beret*).[3] The spelling with ⟨y⟩ is hypercorrect and betrays a false belief that the word was Greek (note that the form *byrrhus* also occurs: *TLL* II.2005.76 f.). It is possible that there was contamination between this and the colour term *byrrus* (*burrus*) (πυρρός), which, though it is attested only in grammarians and glosses, is reflected in Romance,[4] and must therefore have been current.

André (1949, 121) states that the colour term later changed meaning and came to denote a type of garment. He has conflated two distinct words.

3 EPISTVLA

Elsewhere I have argued that under the early Empire *litterae* was used only by a few archaising writers, and that *epistula* was the word in everyday use.[5] The letters support this conclusion. *Epistula* occurs six times (467.24, 25, 468.39, 469.15, 472.15, 17), but there is no example of *litterae*.

4 LONCHA (467.20)

This word (= 'lance') is not quoted by Lewis and Short (1879). *Lancea* alone is used by Vegetius, and it lived on into Romance. *Loncha* was no doubt one of many ephemeral Grecisms (λόγχη) which entered the speech of ordinary

---
[2] See Ernout and Meillet (1959), *s.v.*; Palmer (1954), 53. On the nature of the garment, see Wild (1963).
[3] Meyer-Lübke (1935), 1117 *a*.
[4] Meyer-Lübke (1935), 1117.
[5] Adams (1972), 357.

Roman soldiers,[6] especially those serving in Greek-speaking areas. Many parallels could be quoted. *Capitum*, for example (καπητόν) (= *pabulum*), is found in the *H.A.* and is described by Ammianus as a vulgarism (22.4.9 *pabula iumentorum, quae uulgo dictitant capita*). Vegetius mentions or uses a number of comparable words: e.g. 4.15 *uineas dixerunt ueteres quas nunc militari barbaricoque usu causias uocant* (καυσία); 2.18 *diuersa in scutis signa pingebant, ut ipsi nominant, digmata* (δείγματα); 2.20 *haec ratio apud signiferos, ut nunc dicunt, in cofino seruabatur* (κόφινος); 2.15 *gladios maiores, quos spathas uocant* (σπάθη); 1.5 *proceritatem tironum ad incommam scio semper exactam* (ἔγκομμα).

Later *lancea* was rivalled not by a Greek but by a Frankish word (*speot*, cf. Eng. *spit*.: > OFr. *espiet*).[7]

Conversely, just as Greek-speaking soldiers introduced Greek words into the Roman army, so many Latin military words were borrowed by κοινή Greek.[8] In one of the Greek letters (478.47) φοῦνδιν (= φούνδιον, diminutive of φοῦνδα, *funda*) occurs (see the editors *ad loc.* for the meaning).

5 *OPTIO* (468.53, 54)

The termination *-io* would originally have belonged to words with a root ending in *-i* (e.g. *humilio, macerio, esurio*). But as a result of false analysis of such words the suffix *-io* (which is domiciled mainly in colloquial Latin) emerged as an augmented form of the suffix *-o*. E.g. *morio* < μωρός (note Jerome *Epist.* 2.130.17 *quos moriones uulgo uocant*). *Optio* is formed with the suffix *-io*. We know of many words current in the army which have the suffix *-o* or *-io* (e.g. *tiro, commilito, milito, baro, calo, centurio, commanipulo, latro, pedo*).[9]

---

[6] There are numerous Greek words in the letters: see Calderini (1951), 257.
[7] Elcock (1960), 244.
[8] See Browning (1969), 45 ff.
[9] All these words, and others, are discussed by Fisch (1888).

6 PAVCVM AES (471.10, 13, 31)

In learned prose *paucus* is used in the plural as a quantity word ('few', 'a few'). But words of quantity or number tended to express size as well in Vulgar Latin, just as words of size might express quantity.[10] The use of *paucus* in the singular with the sense 'small', 'a little' (> Fr. *peu*, etc.)[11] is condemned by the *Rhet. Her.* (4.45) in reference to the expression *pauco sermone*: *abusio est quae uerbo simili et propinquo pro certo et proprio abutitur, hoc modo*: . . . '*uti pauco sermone*'.

Paucum aes (which is always in quoted speech in 471) was undoubtedly a current colloquialism. It is also found twice in Gellius (9.4.5, 20.1.31).[12]

7 FORTIS

Fortis seems to be used at 467.2 of health: *op[to te] fortem . . . esse.* This usage is found mainly under the Empire (*TLL* vi.1.1148.37 ff.): e.g. *Vet. Lat.* Tob. 7: 4 *fortis est et uiuit* = ζῇ καὶ ὑγιαίνει (quoted at *TLL* vi.1.1148.65). Earlier *firmus* was preferred (*TLL* vi.1.814.59 ff.).[13]

8 IACEO

Terentianus' illness is referred to in guarded terms in the Latin letters: 468.13 *me iacentem in liburna sublata mi s[unt]*; 21 *modo si non iacu[i]sse, speraba me pluriam tibi missiturum* (cf. 5395.4, 8). Illness, and particularly serious illness, is one of the subjects which attract euphemisms in many languages.[14] *Iaceo* is one such euphemism which turns up in writings of various types (*TLL* vii.1.13.12 ff.): e.g. Cic. *Fam.*

[10] See, e.g., Ernout (1954), 210.   [11] Meyer-Lübke (1935), 6303.
[12] See Krebs and Schmalz (1905), ii, 259.
[13] For the relationship between *fortis* and *firmus* in late Latin, see Adams (1976), 109.
[14] See Löfstedt (1959), 186 f., for a few Latin examples.

9.20.3 *ne ego te iacente bona tua comedim*; cf. Celsus 3.19.3. There are also examples in poetry, where euphemisms are particularly favoured.

As a rough parallel we might mention the unwillingness to state openly that a physician was treating a person for an illness. The euphemisms *uiso* and *uisito* = 'treat' are both attested, the latter particularly often in the medical work of Theodorus Priscianus (e.g. 2.6, 7, 13, 18).

9 *ADIVTO*

Adiuto is one of the words which must have been in regular spoken use from the period of early Latin through to the Romance languages, though rarely surfacing in the literature. It is found in Plautus and Terence, and also a few times in early tragedy, but only once in Cicero, and then in the letters (frg. *ad Q. Axium* 2). It has many reflexes in Romance,[15] whereas *adiuuo*, which is more common in extant literature, does not survive. The evidence of our letters, in which *adiuto* occurs twice (468.41, 471.28) but *adiuuo* only once (470.11), combines with that of Petronius (see 62.11) to establish a continuity between old Latin and the Vulgar Latin of the Empire in this respect.

10 *VENIO*

Eo is used only once in the letters, and then in a polysyllabic form (471.10 *ibo*). There are, however, a number of examples of *uenio*, some of which are superficially odd: (*a*) 471.22 *factum est illi uenire Alexandrie*; (*b*) 24 f. *spec[t]emus illum dum uenit et uen[i]o tequm*; (*c*) 31 f. *ut possim uenire con rebus meis Alexandrie*; (*d*) 34 f. *mater ma . . . uendedi lentiamina [u]t ueniam Alexandrie*.

Since Terentianus is not at Alexandria, it might be thought that in most of these passages *eo* should have been used instead of *uenio*. Cf. 471.14 f. *se exiturum Alexandrie* and 26

[15] Meyer-Lübke (1935), 172.

Saturninus iam paratus erat exire, where the contexts are much the same as those of the above passages. But it is one thing to say that *eo* could have been substituted for *uenio* and another to say that it should.[16] There is often a choice open to a writer between 'come' and 'go', *eo* and *uenio*. In all the above passages the action of travelling could have been viewed from its starting point, and hence *eo* would have been possible in every case. But *uenio* does not refer merely to arrival, i.e. to an action seen at its point of completion. It can imply that the addressee, unlike the speaker, is at the point of destination and that the speaker will himself be there at some time in the future ('I shall come to the office tomorrow'). Or it may imply that the speaker, along with the addressee, will at a future time be at a certain point of destination at which neither is present at the time of utterance ('I shall come with you tomorrow to the office'). The use of *uenio* in all the above passages can be explained from its possession of these functions. We do not know where the addressee of the letter is, but it must be assumed that he is at Alexandria. If so sentences (*a*) and (*d*) fall into the first of the two classes we have noted above (the addressee is at the point of destination, though the speaker himself is not). The two examples would be anomalous only if the addressee were at some place other than Alexandria. (Note that at 472.9 the father of Terentianus, who is the usual addressee of the letters, states explicitly that he is at Alexandria.)

The other two examples fall into the second category above. The speaker, like the addressee, is going to the point of destination. This is quite explicit in sentence (*b*), and it is clear from the context in the other case. The person of whom Terentianus is making demands is about to leave: 26 *Saturninus iam paratus erat exire illa die qu[a]ndo tam magna lites factam est*. Cf. his remark to Terentianus at 33 (*ueni, dicet, Alexandrie et dabo t[i]bi*), an invitation for Terentianus to accompany him.

---

[16] For *uenio* see also Adams (1976), 110 f.

11 *PALPO* (467.17)

With the metaphorical sense ('flatter', 'lead on') in which Terentianus uses it (*nẹ tịḅ[i] pareaṃ a spe ạṃạṛ[a] parp̣a[tum] ụagari quasi fugitiuom*), *palpo* seems to be confined to comedy (Plaut. *Merc.* 169), satire (Lucilius 883, Horace *Sat.* 2.1.20) and Cicero's letters (*Att.* 9.9.1, *Fam.* 10.33.2). It must have been a colloquialism.[17]

12 *PONO*

The editors state that *postae* at 467.23 (*bracae autem nouae postae sunt*) is used for *depositae*. But the original sense of *pono* was 'lay aside' (whence 'store'). Cf. Plaut. *Cist.* 784 *ubi id erit factum, ornamenta ponent*; *Pers.* 363 *dum tunicas ponit, quanta adficitur miseria.* Cf. too the technical term *arma ponere*. The original meaning had obviously not been lost in spoken Latin.

13 *INVENIO, REPERIO*

Inuenio occurs seven times (468.44, 469.7, 16, 471.19, 472.7, 10, 13), but *reperio* only once, and then in the letter of Tiberianus (472.19 f.). The currency of the former in ordinary speech is thus confirmed.[18]

14 *PRAEFVERVNT*

The editors note that this verb 'is given a meaning normally associated only with the adjective *praesens*' at 471.18: *quo tempus autem ueni omnia praefuerunt*. For the acquisition by a verb of a new sense derived from that of a related adjective we might compare the use of *supersto* = 'survive' (cf. *super-*

---

[17] Cf. the vulgarism *palpo* (= 'flatterer') used by Persius (5.176). See Fisch (1888), 81.
[18] See Löfstedt (1911), 232 ff.

stes) in late Latin (there is an example in Ennodius; cf. *CIL* III.12478 *filios superstantis*).

15 PVPLICIVM (468.58)

The adjective *pūblicus* is not related etymologically to *populus* (cf. *pubes*). Spellings with ⟨p⟩ for ⟨b⟩ are due to popular etymology. Cf. Cavenaile (1958), 193.1 Πουπλίῳ, Plaut. *Rud.* 572 *puplicum*.

Finally, on the vulgarism *pluriam* (468.22), see the comprehensive discussion by Lebek (1971).

VI CONCLUSION

We have seen enough linguistic unity to show that the letters were not composed by the various scribes. Terentianus must have dictated them. The following mannerisms are worth noting. *Ille* is preferred to the other demonstratives throughout (III.2.i). Verbs of saying are constantly used in the present historic (III.3.ii). The present participle is avoided in all of the letters (III.3.v). Only one particle (*autem*) is employed with any frequency: various others of equal frequency in other works are absent (III.7). The ablative absolute is avoided (III.8). *Scias* is always used as an introductory formula rather than possible alternatives such as *scito* or *scire te uolo* (both of which are found in Rustius Barbarus: see Cavenaile (1958), 303.14, 306.2; cf. the Greek formula γεινώσκειν σε θέλω used by Terentianus at 476.5) (III.9). And a distinction is observed between the construction employed with positive verbs of saying and that with *nego* (III.9).

Stylistic affectation is not a characteristic of the letters, but the orthography is often learned. The graphemes ⟨k⟩ and ⟨q⟩ are artificially distinguished in accordance with a rule which must have been widely taught in the schools (II.2.vi). Indeed, ⟨q⟩ is written before ⟨u⟩ throughout, despite the fact that the letters cover a considerable time span and were put into writing by different scribes. The spellings *saluom*, etc., and *quominos* (II.1.i) further indicate the conservative habits of schoolmasters in this distant part of the Empire, if we can assume that the scribes learnt to write Latin in Egypt rather than in Italy.[1] Another 'correct' spelling is *mihi*, which alter-

---

[1] The Grecising spellings *nostrous* (see above, II.1.ii) and perhaps *illan*

nates with the phonetically determined *mi* from letter to letter. In this case it is possible that scribal practice varied (for another possibility, see above, II.1.v). It is of note that *mi* is found thirteen times, *mihi* never, in the letters of Rustius Barbarus. *Mihi* was undoubtedly learned.

The only cases of learned or artificial Latin that we have identified are the position of *dicebat* (469.12) after its dependent construction (III.9, IV.5), the archaism *siluit* at 471.15, and its position after the acc. + infin. (III.9, IV.5). It might conceivably be argued that the use both of the acc. + infin. instead of object (*quod*) clauses (III.9), and of the classical case inflections instead of prepositional expressions (III.1.i) was learned, but the existing evidence would not justify such a view.

Since Terentianus was a Greek-speaker, certain items in the Latin letters are readily understandable: the high incidence of Greek words, and in particular the use of *loncha* for the existing Latin word *lancea* (v.4), the construction *factum est* with dat. + infin. (III.9), and above all the order VO in subordinate clauses (IV.1). So the consonant cluster in *sitlas* might have been more readily tolerated by a Greek than a Latin speaker (II.2.vii).

It has been assumed throughout that Tiberianus was the father of Terentianus, as Terentianus implies a number of times. But this assumption involves a difficulty. At 471.21 Terentianus refers to a certain Ptolemaeus as his father. Youtie and Winter (1951, 17) argue plausibly as follows: 'The partial identity of name between Claudius Tiberianus and Claudius Terentianus suggests that they are in reality father and son, and this view is supported by the character of the correspondence, in which nothing betrays a less intimate relationship. In all likelihood, *pater* is applied to Ptolemaeus only as a term of respect' (cf. 30 f.).

If this view is accepted, it is worthwhile to speculate briefly about the character of Tiberianus' family. It has been noted

(III.2.i) suggest that the scribes were native Greek-speakers born in Egypt rather than Italians.

that, while Terentianus' Latin is highly vulgar and possibly marked by Greek interference, that of Tiberianus exhibits greater learning (I.1.ii). It is possible that Tiberianus was an immigrant from Italy (we know that he had been a legionary: see 469.24 and the editors *ad loc.*) who had settled in Egypt and married a Greek-speaker. His son Terentianus would have acquired a spoken form of Latin with Grecising elements, while employing Greek as his usual language.

Some such hypothesis is required to explain a curious circumstance. The first two letters (as Davies (1973) emphasises) describe Terentianus' efforts to join the Roman armed services in Egypt. He was therefore at one stage a resident in Egypt who was not yet in the army. It calls for explanation that a local inhabitant should write to his own father in fluent Latin. A full Greek would certainly not have done so. Nor is it plausible that his father was a Greek who had picked up some Latin in the army and imparted it to his offspring. A native Greek who had learnt Latin would either not have spoken the language at all to his offspring, or at least would not have used it with sufficient regularity to transmit a complete fluency. And his son would not have been likely to address him in Latin. The obvious solution is that Terentianus was the son of an Italian who, even if fluent in Greek, would naturally have used Latin to his children.

The letters provide important evidence of various kinds. Since, for example, the masculine dative *illi* is in use but there is a remodelled feminine *illei*, we are able to modify the traditional explanation of the form *illaei* (III.2.i). It is now placed beyond doubt that *ille* had replaced *is* by the early Empire in Vulgar Latin (III.2.i). We have seen in the rarity both in the letters and at Pompeii of accusative singulars in ⟨-u⟩ grounds for believing that the restructuring of the vowel system, whatever its details (see Appendix), began in the front rather than the back vowels (II.2.i). The restructuring apparent at Pompeii can no longer be ascribed to possible substrate influence,[2] now that it is in evidence so soon after in

[2] See Spence (1965), 12.

CONCLUSION 87

the Roman army in Egypt. There is enough new evidence bearing on the neutralisation of /d/ and /t/ in final position in monosyllables to hint strongly at the form which this neutralisation took (II.2.ii). Either *tempus* had already been fossilised as an indicator of point of time, or the existence of a new type of unconstrued nominative must be admitted (III.1.iii). The usual account of the development of the accusative of price should be revised (III.1.iv). Finally, the letters give the first substantial indication of the extent to which sub-literate word order was diverging from that of educated Latin in anticipation of Romance patterns, and in particular of the shift from patterns of an OV type to those of a VO type which had taken place in popular speech.

I conclude with a list of passages where the text as it is printed by the editors could be improved:

    467.5   retain *anaboladum* (II.1.v)
    470.11   retain *aduuabat* (II.1.v)
    471.19   retain *dende* (II.1.v)
    471.34   retain *ma* (II.1.v)
    471.17   retain *tus* (II.1.v)
    471.30   retain *sum* (II.1.v)
    471.34   retain *uendedi* (II.2.ii)
    471.19   retain *pos* (II.2.ii)
    471.12   read *hinc ed inde* (p. 7, n. 5)
    468.40   retain *ualunt* (III.3.i)
    471.15   retain *quam* (III.4)
    471.16   remove ⟨*dedit*⟩ (III.4)
    471.24   remove ⟨*dicit*⟩ (III.9)

In addition final ⟨m⟩ and initial ⟨h⟩ should not be supplied when omitted.

APPENDIX
Changes in the vowel system

It has recently been argued by Spence (1965)[1] that the orthographic confusion of ⟨e⟩ and ⟨i⟩ and ⟨o⟩ and ⟨u⟩ at Pompeii was not due to the merger of the /ē/ and /i/ and /ō/ and /u/ phonemes, and that quantitative oppositions had not by this time decayed. He sees the starting point of the revolution in the vowel system as the widening of the allophonic range of the short phonemes. Thus a qualitative change in /i/ might cause it to be perceived by some speakers as an allophene [ẹ]. 'Length not normally being noted in the orthography, ẹ̆ (<ĭ) would not be distinguished in spelling from ẹ̄ (<ē)' (12). The next stage he describes thus: 'where the actualisation of /ĭ/ and /ŭ/ was allowed to drift to phonetic ẹ and ọ, it seems inevitable that they should eventually be correlated with /ē/ and /ō/' (13).

Coleman (1971) argues that the monophthongisation of /ae/ took the form [ae] > [ɛ̄] > [ẹ]. He shows that in inscriptions ⟨ae⟩ is hypercorrectively written both for classical /ĕ/ (i.e. [ɛ]) and /ē/ (i.e. [ẹ̄]). His explanation of these phenomena (190) is that in a transitional period the reflex of /ae/ shared quantity with /ē/ and quality with /ĕ/ (i.e. that it was [ɛ̄]). Now at Pompeii we find ⟨ae⟩ for both /ĕ/ and /ē/ (Väänänen (1966), 24 f.). It would therefore seem that quantitative oppositions still existed at the time: otherwise why should ⟨ae⟩ be written for classical /ē/, from which it undoubtedly differed in quality? The obvious conclusion is that spellings of the type ⟨e⟩ for /i/ found at Pompeii could not represent a merger of the phonemes /ē/ and /i/ caused by the loss of phonemic quantity.

[1] Since this book went to press the following articles relevant to the Vulgar Latin vowel system have appeared: N. C. W. Spence, 'A further note on the monophthongization of Latin *ae*', *T.Ph.S.* (1975), 81 ff.; R. G. G. Coleman, 'The monophthongization of Latin *ae*: a reply', *ibid.*, 86 ff.

APPENDIX: CHANGES IN THE VOWEL SYSTEM 89

Against this it must be urged that excessive weight is given to inverse spellings, which may be haphazard and irrational. It is difficult to believe that ⟨ae⟩ would be associated with a phonetic realisation in writers' minds. Since it existed only as a grapheme on the written page, it would surely be associated with the grapheme ⟨e⟩ with which it was in alternation. Now after phonemic quantity was lost, ⟨e⟩ had two values, [ẹ] and [ę]. Therefore as a hyperurbanism ⟨ae⟩, because it alternated in writing with ⟨e⟩, might be written for /ẹ/ (<classical /ē/) or /ę/ (<classical /e/). That the orthography ⟨ae⟩ for classical /ē/ need not imply that the quantitative system was intact is proved conclusively by the fact that it was still common at a very late period (e.g. in the sixth and seventh centuries), when phonemic quantity had certainly been effaced (see, e.g., B. Löfstedt (1961), 101 f.).

Spence gives no conclusive evidence in support of his view. Moreover when /i/ developed an allophone [ẹ], the phoneme /i/ would now have consisted of two allophones, [i] and [ẹ]. After [ẹ] was correlated with /ē/, what happened to [i]?

Nor is it necessary to maintain that, if the aberrational spellings at Pompeii represented the merger of /ē/ and /i/, the initial stages of the process (i.e. the loss of quantitative distinctions) would have to be placed as far back as the second century B.C. (Spence (1965), 8). The loss of phonemic quantity could be concurrent with the convergence: as soon as quantity was neglected in, say, unstressed syllables, /ē/ and /i/ would no longer be distinct. The following stages would be equally consistent with the few inadequate facts which we have at our disposal: (*a*) the coexistence of quantitative and qualitative distinctions, the long vowels being closer and occupying a wider area of articulation (see Allen (1965), 47 ff.; (1973), 131 ff.); (*b*) the neglect of quantitative distinctions, first in unstressed, and then in stressed syllables; (*c*) the rise to phonemic status of the already existing qualitative distinctions, accompanied by the merger of /ē/ and /i/ and /ō/ and /u/.

MODERN WORKS CITED

Adams, J. N. (1972), 'The language of the later books of Tacitus' *Annals*', C.Q., n.s., 22, 350 ff.
— (1976), *The Text and Language of a Vulgar Latin Chronicle (Anonymus Valesianus II)* (Supplement 36, *B.I.C.S.*), London.
— (forthcoming, *a*), 'A typological approach to Latin word order', *I.F.*
— (forthcoming, *b*), 'The Vulgar Latin of Egypt in the early Empire', *Aufstieg und Niedergang der römischen Welt*.
Allen, W. Sidney (1965), *Vox Latina*, Cambridge.
— (1973), *Accent and Rhythm. Prosodic Features of Latin and Greek: a Study in Theory and Reconstruction*, Cambridge.
Anderson, J. M. (1964–65), 'Neutralisation of phonemic opposition in Vulgar Latin', *Romance Notes*, 6, 86 ff.
André, J. (1949), *Étude sur les termes de couleur dans la langue latine*, Paris.
Baehrens, W. A., (1922), *Sprachlicher Kommentar zur vulgärlateinischen Appendix Probi*, Halle.
Battisti, C. (1949), *Avviamento allo studio del latino volgare*, Bari.
Bonfante, G. (1967), 'La lingua delle Atellane e dei Mimi', *Maia*, 19, 3 ff.
Bonnet, M. (1890), *Le Latin de Grégoire de Tours*, Paris.
Bourciez, E. (1946), *Éléments de linguistique romane*, fourth edition, Paris.
Brown, Virginia (1970), 'A Latin letter from Oxyrhynchus', *B.I.C.S.*, 17, 136 ff.
Browning, R. (1969), *Medieval and Modern Greek*, London.
Buck, C. D. (1933), *Comparative Grammar of Greek and Latin*, Chicago, Ill.

Calderini, A. (1951), 'Osservazioni sul latino del P. Mich. VIII, 467–472', *Rendiconti Ist. Lombardo, Classe di lettere e scienze morale e storiche*, 84, 250 ff.
Cameron, A. (1931), 'Latin words in the Greek inscriptions of Asia Minor', *A.J.P.*, 52, 232 ff.
Cameron, A. D. E. (1970), *Claudian. Poetry and Propaganda at the Court of Honorius*, Oxford.
Campanile, E. (1969), 'Valutazione del latino di Britannia', *Studi e saggi linguistici* 9, 87 ff.
— (1971), 'Due studi sul latino volgare: I, Il latino volgare in età repubblicana; II, Il contributo dei testi papiracei alla conoscenza del latino volgare', *L'Italia dialettale*, 34, 1 ff.
Carlton, C. M. (1973), *A Linguistic Analysis of a Collection of Late Latin Documents composed in Ravenna between A.D. 445–700*, The Hague.
Carnoy, A. (1906), *Le Latin d'Espagne d'après les inscriptions*, second edition, Brussels.
Cavenaile, R. (1951), 'Influence latine sur le vocabulaire grec d'Égypte', *Chronique d'Égypte*, 26, 391 ff.
— (1958), *Corpus Papyrorum Latinarum*, Wiesbaden.
Coleman, R. G. G. (1963), 'Two linguistic topics in Quintilian', *C.Q.*, n.s., 13, 1 ff.
— (1971), 'The monophthongization of /ae/ and the Vulgar Latin vowel system', *T.Ph.S.*, 175 ff.
Collingwood, R. G., and Wright, R. P. (1965), *The Roman Inscriptions of Britain*, I, London.
Daris, S. (1960), 'Il lessico latino nella lingua greca d'Egitto', *Aegyptus*, 40, 177 ff.
Davis, R. W. (1973), 'The enlistment of Claudius Terentianus', *B.A.S.P.*, 10, 21 ff.
Diehl, E. (1910), *Vulgärlateinische Inschriften*, Bonn.
Dover, K. J. (1968), *Greek Word Order*, Cambridge.
Elcock, W. D. (1960), *The Romance Languages*, London.
Ernout, A. (1953), *Morphologie historique du latin*, third edition, Paris.
— (1954), *Aspects du vocabulaire latin*, Paris.
Ernout, A., and Meillet, A. (1959), *Dictionnaire étymologique de la langue latine*, fourth edition, Paris.
Ernout, A. and Thomas, F. (1953), *Syntaxe latine*, second edition, Paris.

Exler, F. C. J. (1923), *The Form of the Ancient Greek Letter: a Study in Greek Epistolography*, Washington, D.C.
Fisch, R. (1888), 'Substantiva personalia auf o, onis', *A.L.L.*, 5, 56 ff.
Gaeng, P. A. (1968), *An Enquiry into Local Variations in Vulgar Latin* (University of North Carolina Studies in the Romance Languages and Literatures, 77), Chapel Hill, N.C.
Grandgent, C. H. (1907), *An Introduction to Vulgar Latin*, Boston, Mass.
— (1927), *From Latin to Italian*, Cambridge, Mass.
Greenberg, J. H. (1966), 'Some universals of grammar with particular reference to the order of meaningful elements', in *Universals of Language*, second edition, ed. J. H. Greenberg, Cambridge, Mass.
Gröber, G. (1884), 'Vulgärlateinische Substrate romanischer Wörter', *A.L.L.*, 1, 204 ff., 539 ff.
Hamp, E. P. (1959), 'Final -s in Latin', *C.P.*, 54, 165 ff.
Heraeus, W. (1925), 'Zur neueren Martialkritik', *RhM.*, 74, 314 ff.
Hofmann, J. B. (1951), *Lateinische Umgangssprache*, third edition, Heidelberg.
Hofmann, J. B., and Szantyr, A. (1965), *Lateinische Syntax und Stilistik*, Munich.
Jackson, K. (1953), *Language and History in Early Britain*, Edinburgh.
Josephson, Å. (1950), *Casae Litterarum: Studien zum Corpus Agrimensorum Romanorum*, Uppsala.
Jungemann, F. H. (1955), *La teoría del sustrato y los dialectos hispano-romances y gascones*, Madrid.
Kent, R. G., (1945), *The Sounds of Latin*, third edition, Baltimore, Md.
Krebs, J. P., and Schmalz, J. H. (1905), *Antibarbarus der lateinischen Sprache*, seventh edition, Basel.
Lebek, W. D. (1971), '*Pluria* und *compluria* in lateinischer Sprache und römischer Grammatik', *Rh.M.*, 114, 340 ff.
Lehmann, W. P. (1972), 'Contemporary linguistics and Indo-European studies', *P.M.L.A.*, 87, 976 ff.
— (1974), *Proto-Indo-European Syntax*, Austin, Texas.
Lewis, C. T., and Short, C. (1879), *A Latin Dictionary*, Oxford.
Linde, P. (1923), 'Die Stellung des Verbs in der lateinischen Prosa', *Glotta*, 12, 153 ff.

Lindsay, W. M. (1894), *The Latin Language*, Oxford.
Löfstedt, B. (1961), *Studien über die Sprache der langobardischen Gesetze*, Uppsala.
— (1962), 'Die betonten Hiatusvokale in Wörtern vom Typus *pius, tuus, meus*', *Eranos*, 60, 80 ff.
Löfstedt, E. (1911), *Philologischer Kommentar zur Peregrinatio Aetheriae*, Uppsala.
— (1933–42), *Syntactica: Studien und Beiträge zur historischen Syntax des Lateins*, two vols., Lund.
— (1936), *Vermischte Studien zur lateinischen Sprachkunde und Syntax*, Lund.
— (1959), *Late Latin*, Oslo.
Lyons, J. (1971), *Introduction to Theoretical Linguistics*, Cambridge.
Martinet, A. (1963) [1973], 'Neutralisation' (trans. E. C. Fudge, in *Phonology: Selected Readings*, ed. E. C. Fudge, Penguin, 1973), 74 ff.
Mayser, E. (1906–34), *Grammatik der griechischen Papyri aus der Ptolemäerzeit*, two vols., Berlin and Leipzig.
Meillet, A. (1965), *Aperçu d'une histoire de la langue grecque*, seventh edition, Paris.
Meinersmann, B. (1927), *Die lateinischen Wörter und Namen in den griechischen Papyri*, Leipzig.
Meyer-Lübke, W. (1890–1906), *Grammaire des langues romanes* (trans. E. Rabiet and A. and G. Doutrepont), four vols., Paris.
— (1935), *Romanisches etymologisches Wörterbuch*, third edition, Heidelberg.
Monteil, P. (1974), *Éléments de phonétique et de morphologie du latin*, Paris.
Moulton, J. H. (1908), *A Grammar of New Testament Greek*, third edition, vol. I, Edinburgh.
Neue, F., and Wagener, C. (1892–1905), *Formenlehre der lateinischen Sprache*, four vols., Leipzig and Berlin.
Norberg, D. (1943), *Syntaktische Forschungen auf dem Gebiete des Spätlateins und des frühen Mittellateins*, Uppsala.
Palmer, L. R. (1954), *The Latin Language*, London.
Pighi, G. B. (1964), *Lettere latine d'un soldato di Traiano (P. Mich. 467–472)*, Bologna.
Pirson, J. (1901), *La Langue des inscriptions latines de la Gaule*, Brussels.

Politzer, R. L. (1952), 'On *b* and *v* in Latin and Romance', *Word*, 8, 211 ff.
Pope, M. K. (1934), *From Latin to Modern French*, Manchester.
Ramsden, H. (1963), *Weak-pronoun Position in the Early Romance Languages*, Manchester.
Robins, R. H. (1971), *General Linguistics: an Introductory Survey*, second edition, London.
Rodgers, R. H. (1970), 'From the Tiberianus archive (P. Mich. inv. nr. 5395)', *Z.P.E.*, 5, 91 ff.
Rohlfs, G. (1949–53), *Historische Grammatik der italienischen Sprache und ihrer Mundarten*, three vols., Bern.
— (1969), *Sermo vulgaris Latinus*, third edition, Tübingen.
Safarewicz, J. (1964), 'Sur le développement des consonnes occlusives finales en latin', *Eos*, 54, 99 ff.
Schuchardt, H. (1866–68), *Der Vokalismus des Vulgärlateins*, three vols., Leipzig.
Seelmann, E. (1885), *Die Aussprache des Latein*, Heilbronn.
Sommer, F. (1914), *Handbuch der lateinischen Laut- und Formenlehre*, second and third editions, Heidelberg.
Souter, A. (1949), *A Glossary of Later Latin to 600 A.D.*, Oxford.
Spence, N. C. W. (1965), 'Quantity and quality in the vowel-system of Vulgar Latin', *Word*, 21, 1 ff.
Steen, H. A. (1938), 'Les clichés epistolaires dans les lettres sur papyrus grecques', *Class. et Med.*, 1, 119 ff.
Stefenelli, A. (1962), *Die Volkssprache im Werk des Petron im Hinblick auf die romanischen Sprachen*, Vienna.
Sturtevant, E. H. (1940), *The Pronunciation of Greek and Latin*, second edition, Philadelphia, Pa.
Svennung, J. (1941), *Compositions Lucenses: Studien zum Inhalt, zur Textkritik und Sprache*, Uppsala.
Turner, E. G. (1975), 'Oxyrhynchus and Rome', *H.S.C.P.*, 79, 1 ff.
Uddholm, A. (1953), *Formulae Marculfi: études sur la langue et le style*, Uppsala.
Väänänen, V. (1965), *Étude sur le texte et la langue des Tablettes Albertini*, Helsinki.
— (1966), *Le Latin vulgaire des inscriptions pompéiennes*, third edition, Berlin.
— (1967), *Introduction au latin vulgaire*, second edition, Paris.
Vielliard, J. (1927), *Le Latin des diplômes royaux et chartes privées de l'époque mérovingienne*, Paris.

Weinreich, U. (1953), *Languages in Contact*, New York.
Wild, J. P. W. (1963), 'The *Byrrus Britannicus*', *Ant.*, 37, 193 ff.
Youtie, H. C. (1975), 'ὑπογραφεύς: the social impact of illiteracy in Graeco-Roman Egypt', *Z.P.E.*, 17, 201 ff.
Youtie, H. C., and Winter, J. G. (1951), *Papyri and Ostraca from Karanis (Michigan Papyri VIII)*, Ann Arbor, Mich.

WORD INDEX

This list contains Latin words used by Terentianus. The form given is usually that which appears in the letters.

abs 12
aduuabat (= *adiuuabat*) 19, 87
aiuto (= *adiuto*) 8, 19, 20, 42 (+ dat.), 80
Alexandrie 12, 38
amicla 21
anaboladum (= *anaboladium*) 19, 87
anbobus 25, 45
aspros 21, 76 (= 'cash')
autem 59, 84

benio 31
bia (= *uia*) 31
bolt, boleba 10, 31
byrrus 77

calcio 19, 54 (reflex.)
celerius 58
collexi 53
commandaticiae 8
con (prep.) 10, 25, 36 f.
coplam 21
crebrum (adv.) 56 f.

dalabra (= *dolabra*) 14
daturus est 49
de 36
dende (= *deinde*) 20, 87
domo (= loc.) 38 f.
dum 55

ebinde (wrong reading) 7 n. 5
ed (= *et*) 7 n. 5, 27 f.
emaram (= *emeram*) 13 n. 33
epistula 77

exiendo (= *exeunti*) 54
expediui (= *expetiui*) 31

factum est (+ infin.) 63 f., 85
fiet (= *fit*) 51
fortis 79
fugitiuom 10

glabatulum (=*grabatulum*) 34, 43 f.

hic (demonstr.) 44
hinc ed inde 7 n. 5, 87
hunc (= *hoc*) 44

iaceo 79 f.
ibi (= *iui*) 31
illan 25, 45
ille 44, 84
illec 8, 45
illei (= *illaei*, fem. dat.) 45 ff., 86
illim (adv.) 47
illuc (demonstr.) 43, 45
illunc 45
im (=*in*) 25
imboluclum (=*inuolucrum*) 25, 31, 34
in 36
inpendia 25
inquid (= *inquit*) 28 f.
inuenio 12, 25 (*imbenio*), 82
is 44
Isituchen 45
itarum (= *iterum*) 13
item...quam (correl.) 55 f.
iui (= *ibi*) 31

karissimo 32
karum 32
kasus 32

lentiamina (= *linteamina*) 8, 19
linium (= *lineum*) 19
lites (= *lis*) 42 f.
loncha 77 f., 85

ma (= *mea*) 21, 87
mequm 32
merca 52
mi 20 f., 35, 84 f.
missiturum (= *missurum*) 49 f.
missurus es 49
modo si 55

negabit = *negauit* 31, 48 f.
nese, nesi (= *nisi*) 8
nisi si 55
nostrous (= *nostros*) 13, 45
nouom 10
nullus (= *nemo*) 47 f.

optio 78

palpo 82
parit (= *peperit*) 52
pater 85
paucus (sing.) 79
pauqum 32
perbene (+adv.) 58
pluriam 83
pos (=*post*) 29, 87
posso 11, 52 f.
postae 21, 82
praefuerunt 82
praegnatam 12, 56
pretium (masc. acc.) 44
pro 36
Ptolemes 21

pulbino 11, 31, 37
Puplicium 83

quando 54
qui (= *quis*) 30 n. 112, 47
qumqupibit (= *concupiuit*) 10, 31, 32
quo tempus 39 f., 55, 87
quominos 11, 84
quoniam 55
qurauit 32

reliquid (= *reliquit*) 28 f.
reperio 12, 82

saluom 10, 84
sene (= *sine*) 8
sequrus 32
si 64
siluit 72, 85
singlare 21
sitlas 21, 33 f., 85
sopera 10 f., 36
specto (= *exspecto*) 21 f.
sum (= *suum*) 21, 87

tam magna 56
tequm 32
Turranium 35
tus (= *tuus*) 21, 87

ualunt (= *ualent*) 51, 87
ud (= *ut*) 27 f.
uendidi 8, 29, 87
uenio 80 f.
uetranum 21
uiciturum (= *uicturum*) 49 ff.
uide si 55, 64
uitriae 19, 43 (fem. sing.)

xylesphongium 8

SUBJECT INDEX

ablative 36 f. (with prepp.), 38 f. (= loc.), 42 (of time)
ablative absolute 12, 53, 59, 60 f., 84
accusative 36 f. (prepositional case), 40 ff. (of price), 62 (of exclamation?), 87 (of price)
accusative absolute 59 f.
accusative + infinitive 61 ff., 72 (position)
adjectives 56, 71 (position)
adverbs 47, 56 ff., 72 (position)
anacolouthon 60, 61, 62
analogy 9, 42, 50 (proportional and non-proportional), 54
aphaeresis 21 f.
apposition, partitive 42
archaisms 9 f. (of spelling), 11 (of spelling), 72, 85
aspiration 34 f.
assimilation 13 (vocalic), 14 ff. (vocalic), 25 ff. (of final consonants), 34 (distant)

bilinguals and bilingualism 3 f., 34, 61, 66, 75, 85, 86

comparative, contrastive use of 58
conjunctions 54 f., 64
consonants 22 ff., 48 f., 52
contamination 11, 29, 46, 47, 54, 56, 60, 63, 63 f., 77
contraction of vowels 20 f., 84 f.

date of letters 3
dative 42 (with *adiuto*), 45 ff. (*illaei*)

dative + infinitive 63 f.
demonstrative pronouns 43, 44 ff., 69 f., 84, 86
deponent verb 52 (active use)
diphthongs 11 ff.
direct and indirect quotation 62

Egypt, Latin of 2 f.
ellipse 55 f., 62, 76
epistolary formulae 4 f., 56, 62, 68, 72, 74, 84
euphemism 79 f.

fossilised accusatives 40, 41, 87

gemination 35
gender 43 f.
genitive 43 (of material), 46 f. (*illaeius*), 67 (position), 70 f. (position)
gerund 54 (abl.)
Greek interference 3, 13, 21, 34, 45, 57, 64, 66, 68 f., 70, 74, 75, 77 f., 85 f.

hiatus 18 ff.
hyperurbanism 5, 11, 25, 45, 61, 77

indicative and subjunctive mood 55, 63, 64
indirect commands 72 (position)
indirect questions 64, 72 (position)
infinitive 51 (pres. = fut. pass), 63 (replacing *ut*), 71 (position), 85

Koine Greek 3, 7, 38, 48, 52 n. 54, 61, 66 ff. (word order), 78

literary Latin 63, 85 (*cf.* 'Tiberianus, Latin of')
locative 38 f.

negation, pleonastic 65
neutralisation 26 ff., 87
nominative 42 f., unconstrued: 39 f., 43, 87

object position 68 ff., 74 f.
Old Latin 13, 29, 38, 42, 45, 47, 55, 57, 58, 64, 67, 73, 80
orthography 5, 7, 9, 10, 11, 12, 13 n. 31, 19, 20, 24, 26, 28, 29, 30, 32 f., 45 n. 33, 77, 84 f.

palatalisation 19 f.
participles 49 ff. (perf., fut.), 53 f. (pres.), 84 (pres.)
particles 59, 84
Petronius 1, 38, 39, 41, 42, 44, 55, 56, 57, 59, 65, 67, 80
pleonasm 65
Pompeian inscriptions 1, 9, 11, 18, 19, 22, 27, 32, 45
popular etymology 83

prepositions 36 ff., 72 (position of prep. expressions)
prothesis 22

recomposition 8
reflexive verbs 54
relative clauses 72 f. (position)
Rustius Barbarus 2, 5, 9, 84, 85

scribes 3, 4, 49, 84 f.
subordinate clauses, verb position in 69, 70, 73 f., 85
superlatives, periphrastic 56, 58
syncope 10 f., 21, 33, 34, 76

tense 48 ff. (fut.), 50 (perf.), 51 f. (pres. hist.), 52 (perf.), 53 (perf.), 84 (pres. hist.)
Tiberianus, Latin of 12, 21, 50, 60 f., 82, 86
typology, and word order 66 ff.

verb position 73 f. (*cf.* 'subordinate clauses')
voicing of intervocalic stops 30 f.
vowels 7 ff., 48, 52, 86, 88 f.

Wackernagel's Law 69
word order 5 n. 18, 62, 63, 64, 66 ff., 85, 87